Europe and the World

In the same series
Europe and the World, 1300–1763

Europe
and the
World, 1763–1960

David Sturdy, Ph.D.

GILL AND MACMILLAN

First Published in 1971

Gill and Macmillan Ltd
2 Belvedere Place
Dublin 1
and in London through association with
Macmillan and Co Ltd

© *David Sturdy, Ph.D.*

Cover design by Cor Klaasen

7171 0489 3

Produced in Ireland at Richview Press Limited.

Contents

Preface

With a subject as broad as that covered in this volume it was necessary to be selective in the issues discussed. Some I have analysed in more detail than others, but I hope that the lists of things to do and of further reading will suggest lines of more extensive study on matters with which I have not dealt in detail. In my approach to this book I have tried to introduce students to the concept that on many episodes of man's past historians disagree over questions of interpretation; certain examples are specifically pointed out in the text. I have tried to do more than simply provide students with the barest amount of information necessary for examinations, and have attempted to take them more deeply into historical problems.

Several people have read and made invaluable comments upon this book, and my thanks are especially due to Miss H Hamerstein, Dr A C Clarke, and Dr L M Cullen of Trinity College, Dublin.

David Sturdy

Introduction

In the mid-eighteenth century life was little different from that of previous centuries so far as most Europeans were concerned. They were still ruled by kings, the Dutch and the Swiss being among the few exceptions. Most of them were peasants, for in western Europe peasants made up about 80% of the population, and in central and eastern Europe, over 90%. Many of these peasants paid feudal dues to their overlords. When they worked the land they used techniques that were practised in earlier centuries. Illiteracy was common; so was bad health; infant mortality was high. In all these ways, and in others, life in the 1750s closely resembled life in the 1650s, 1550s, and 1450s. Imagine an eighteenth century person on a journey across time, send him back two centuries into the 1500s, and in the lives of most people he would discover few aspects that were strange or unfamiliar.

If, on the other hand, he were carried 200 years into the future and saw Europe in the 1950s, he would be utterly astonished at the new civilisation. For one thing, the great states of his day either have vanished like the Habsburg empire, diminished in international authority like Britain, France and Spain, or have been transformed like Prussia and Russia. Such monarchs as remain are but nominal heads of state. Europe's status in the world has declined. Of all the continents she does not possess the largest population, she is not the wealthiest, she no longer commands the most formidable armed might, and her once vast overseas empires have almost vanished. Yet life for the average European is richer than ever before. The population has grown; Europeans are well educated, healthy, expect a long life, eat well, dress well, have an increasing amount of leisure time, and regard as commonplace household gadgets that were undreamed of in the eighteenth century. It does not require a huge effort of imagination to appreciate the immense number of changes that have occurred in European life from about 1750 to the present.

Here, indeed, is the main theme of our study: change. In the last 200 years European society has been subjected to a host of forces that have produced a civilisation radically different from that of the past. It is our purpose to study these forces, to examine their effect upon each other, and to estimate their influence upon Europe. Oddly enough the place to begin is America, for it was there that the social, economic and political forces that led to turmoil in Europe first made their dramatic impact through the American Revolution.

1

The American Revolution

Britain and North America

The Seven Years war (1756–63) ended with the peace of Paris. In the peace terms France lost large areas of North America to Britain. As a result, British possessions there extended from Newfoundland to Florida and inland as far as the Ohio and Mississippi rivers. Up to the 1750s Britain's thirteen North American colonies had been virtually self-governing, while the Navigation Acts were haphazardly enforced. The Navigation Acts had been passed between 1660 and 1696, and decreed that certain basic colonial products such as tobacco, sugar, rice and indigo, must be shipped either to Britain or to other British colonies; also, all goods imported into the colonies must come through Britain. In fact the North American colonies did as much trade with southern Europe and the French West Indies as they did with Britain.

After 1763 British policy tried to alter this state of affairs by subjecting the colonies to stiffer political and economic control. One reason for this was financial. The costs of government and administration were growing, while Britain's involvement in the war of the Austrian Succession (1740–8) and in the Seven Years war had seriously drained her financial resources. The government badly needed cash, and in an effort to raise more

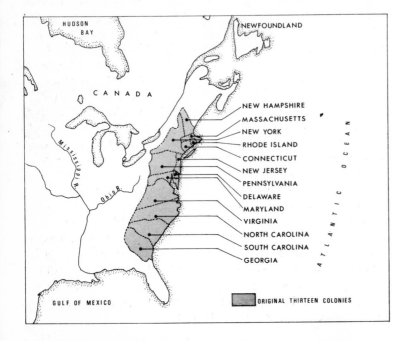

Britain's thirteen North American colonies.

King George III (1738–1820).

money decided that the colonies must pay more taxes. Another reason was commercial. British merchants and government officials resented the North American colonies' trade outside the empire. They saw it as trade lost to Britain, therefore as wealth lost to Britain, and wished to see North American merchants contribute more to British trade. Finally, there was a military motive. The British feared that the French would try not only to reconquer their lost territories but seize the British colonies as well. Therefore a strong British army was needed in the colonies to defend them, and the government considered that the colonists should help to meet the costs involved.

British Policy in the 1760s

When the British government decided to tighten its grip on the economic and political affairs of its North American colonies, this meant achieving certain practical goals. The trade and navigation laws must be enforced to aid British commerce; taxes must be raised to pay for the administration of the colonies; expansion westwards and trade with the Indians must be controlled so that Britain would reap the benefit; the colonies must accept that Parliament was responsible for major decisions upon their future; quarters and provisions must be found for the army.

In order to fulfil these aims, eight important Acts were passed by the British Parliament between 1763 and 1767:

1763—the Proclamation (the 'Royal Order') put Indian affairs and all territory west of a certain line into the hands of the British government.

1764—the Revenue Act (the 'Sugar Act') improved the colonial customs service and raised money to pay for military bases in North America.

1764—the Currency Act stopped the colonies from issuing paper money.

1765—the Stamp Act raised money for the administration and for the maintenance of troops in the colonies by imposing a stamp duty on such items as newspapers, wills, licences and contracts.

1765—the Quartering Act made the colonies provide supplies for British troops living in barracks belonging to the colonies.

1766—the Declaratory Act applied the Declaratory Act (Ireland) of 1719 to the colonies and announced that Parliament was responsible for passing laws concerning them.

1767—the Customs Collecting Act established British agents in the colonies to collect customs duties and other taxes.

1767—the Revenue Act imposed duties on certain British goods, including tea, which were imported into the colonies; the funds thus raised were for the administration of the colonies.

American Opposition to the Stamp Act

A programme like this would have produced protests among the American colonists at the best of times, but it was particularly

Colonists demonstrate their opposition to the Stamp Act by burning stamps in a Boston street.

bound to do so in the 1760s. The colonies were suffering an economic depression which had led to widespread unemployment in the towns and along the coast. The governing bodies of several colonies were heavily in debt because of their involvement in the Seven Years war. Tense political rivalries existed, for many settlers resented the political power of the great merchants and planters. Given the extent of these internal colonial problems, the British were playing with fire when they tried to subject the Americans to closer control.

As the series of Acts was passed by Parliament there was at first grumbling among the colonists, then louder protests, and finally outrage. The leading merchants and planters were especially opposed to British policy, for they saw it as an attack upon their domination of the economic and political life of the colonies. They whipped up popular antagonism, called meetings to protest against the Acts, encouraged the press to condemn British policy, and turned a sympathetic eye on mobs who demonstrated against British officials.

The measure that led to the widest disorders was the Stamp Act, for it affected everybody. All over the colonies there were demonstrations and riots, often directed against the agents who had been appointed to collect the stamp duty. There exists an account of demonstrations against the Boston stamp agent and two of his supporters, Martin Howard and Dr. Moffat. A mob hanged them in effigy and scrawled insults across the dummies. On the agent's dummy was written, 'the stamp man', while Howard's effigy bore the words, 'that fawning, insidious, infamous miscreant and paracide [parasite], Martinius Scliberius'; the words on the doctor's image called him, 'that infamous, miscreated, leering Jacobite doctor Murfy [Moffat]'. Later that day the crowd attacked Howard's home and, according to an observer, 'broke every window in his house, frames and all; likewise chairs, tables, pictures, and everything they could come across . . . When they found they had entirely demolished all his furniture and done what damage they could, they left his house and proceeded to Dr. Moffat's where they behaved much in the same manner'.

Opposition to the Stamp Act was also expressed through more formal, though just as serious, means. Merchants made agreements to boycott British goods. Bands known as 'the Sons of Liberty' were formed whose purpose was to resist 'despotic' acts by the British government. Many town councils met and condemned the Stamp Act. Representatives from nine of the colonies met in New York to discuss the Act, and their resolutions not only denounced it but were to provide slogans for the anti-British movement during the next few years. The resolutions stated that it was, 'the undoubted right of Englishmen, that no taxes should be imposed on them, but with their own consent, given personally, or by their representatives.' They continued that, 'the people of these colonies are not . . . represented in the House of Commons in Great Britain', and that furthermore, 'no taxes ever have been, or can be constitutionally imposed on them, but by their respective legislature.' The resolutions concluded therefore that, 'the said Act, [the Stamp Act] and several other Acts . . . have a manifest tendency to subvert the rights and liberties of the colonists.' The Stamp Act Congress (as the New York meeting is known), hence gave a clear definition of the reasons why the Act had met with such antagonism, and from it came the famous colonial cry, 'no taxation without representation'.

The Repeal of the Stamp Act: the Declaratory Act

Confronted by this barrage of protest, the British backed down and Parliament repealed the Stamp Act in 1766. This was not

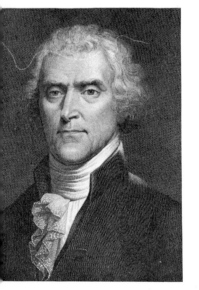

Thomas Jefferson (1743–1826). A fervent patriot, he chaired the committee that drew up the Declaration of Independence; during his active political career he became president of the U.S.A. from 1801–9.

Philadelphia in the eighteenth century.

a full retreat, however, for on the same day it passed the Declaratory Act which insisted that, 'the colonies and plantations in America have been, are, and of right ought to be, subordinate unto, and dependent upon the imperial Crown and Parliament of Great Britain'. It added that the British government, 'had, hath, and of right ought to have, full power and authority to make laws and statutes of sufficient force and validity to bind the colonies and people of America, subjects of the Crown of Great Britain, in all cases whatsoever'.

Here, then, was the position in 1766, and the position as it remained until the revolution. The British insisted that full sovereignty over the colonies lay with Parliament (even though the colonists were not represented there). The Americans argued that sovereignty must be shared with them. The cards were now on the table.

The Patriots

So far there had been no talk of revolution, but in the later 1760s 'popular' or 'patriotic' parties grew, some of which advocated independence. Some of their leaders, like Thomas Jefferson and Samuel Adams, were to play a prominent part in American affairs. Support for the patriots came partly from merchants and planters, but above all from the unemployed in the towns. It was for this reason that they were strongest in the four largest towns, Philadelphia, New York, Charleston and Boston.

There were two grievances in particular upon which the patriotic parties played. One was the presence of British troops. The patriots encouraged the Americans to make life as uncomfortable as possible for the troops, and exploited the uproar caused by the 'Boston massacre'. British soldiers had arrived in Boston in 1768, and from the start had been subjected to insults. There were delays in quartering them, the press complained about them, in the streets they were jeered and pelted with dirt. Trouble came to a head on 5 March 1770 when some soldiers killed four young Bostonians. All over the colonies public

Samuel Adams (1722–1803). An early advocate of American independence; he was responsible for founding the Boston correspondence committee in 1772, and he took part in the Continental Congresses; he was one of the signatories of the Declaration of Independence.

A street scene including the Old State House in eighteenth-century Boston

opinion exploded and the patriots held up the 'massacre' as another example of British brutality.

The other grievance that played into the hands of the patriots was popular resentment at the growing efficiency of the customs service. The most spectacular demonstration against the payment of customs duties occurred in Rhode Island in 1772. So infuriated were the inhabitants that they seized a British warship, the *Gaspee*, and destroyed it. This was no action by a minority group; large numbers of people were involved and there was

The port of Boston at the end of the eighteenth century.

The Boston massacre by Paul Revere (1735–1818). Revere was the character in Longfellow's poem, 'The Landlord's Tale of Paul Revere's Ride', who rode from Charleston to Lexington and Lincoln in order to rouse the colonists against the British troops who were going to Concord.

outspoken public support for it. The resentment felt by the Rhode Islanders was to be found throughout the colonies, and more and more people joined the ranks of the patriots.

What the patriotic parties most needed was unity. This was achieved through 'correspondence societies'. The first was founded in Virginia at the suggestion of Thomas Jefferson, Patrick Henry and Richard Henry Lee, and the other colonies quickly followed suit. The purpose of the correspondence societies was to keep each other informed of their activities, but above all to acquire information about the British government's plans for the colonies and to spread it among the societies. News from Britain was sent by correspondents there such as Benjamin Franklin and John Wilkes. Through the correspondence societies the patriots were able (as the Virginia correspondence society put it), 'to RESENT IN ONE BODY any steps that may be taken by the administration to deprive ANY ONE OF US of the least particle of our rights and liberties'.

The 'Boston Tea Party' and its Results

Since the uproar over the Stamp Act the British had tried to avoid provoking the colonies. Nevertheless, because the British East India Company had heavy debts and a surplus of tea, Parliament tried to aid it by the Tea Act of 1773. This Act (which applied to Ireland as well as to America) gave the company the right to send tea directly to the colonies and sell it there; it was to be free of all duties except the import duty of threepence per pound. The Act made the company's tea very

The Boston Tea Party.

Benjamin Franklin (1706–90).
A distinguished philosopher and
scientist as well as statesman;
in 1766 he appeared before the
British House of Commons and
pleaded for a change in policy;
he was a member of the Second
Continental Congress and of the
committee that drafted the
Declaration of Independence.

cheap, cheaper indeed than smuggled tea. Parliament hoped
that the East India Company would consequently enjoy a
greater share of the colonial market and thus be helped out of
its financial difficulties.

The patriots and public opinion as a whole were enraged.
They saw it as an extension of the tea policy of 1767, as legislation without representation, as an attack on colonial liberties.
Again there were meetings, demonstrations and protests, and
as usual Boston was involved. The first tea ships arrived there
in November 1773, and on 16 December a gang of Bostonians
disguised as Indians boarded the ships and dumped the tea into
the harbour.

When Parliament heard of the protests, and especially of the
'Boston Tea Party', it decided to apply the heavy hand. It closed
the port of Boston until the tea should be paid for; the royal
governor of Massachusetts was given increased political
authority while that of the colonists was reduced; the governors
of all the colonies were given the right to seize vacant property
and to house troops there; British officials accused of crime in
Massachusetts were allowed to be tried in another colony or in
England if they could not be sure of a fair trial in Massachusetts.

This tough line further infuriated the colonists and there was
now open talk of independence. The Quebec Act, passed by
Parliament in 1774, added fuel to the flames. It concerned the
former French Canada and guaranteed its religion, language
and institutions; in addition Quebec was now to be governed by
an assembly appointed by Parliament. The patriots denounced

The First Continental Congress, 5 September 1774.

the Act as a dangerous move. The fact that Quebec was to be governed by an appointed assembly, and not by one elected by the French Canadians, raised fears that some day the English-speaking colonies would be governed in the same way.

The Continental Congress and the Declaration of Independence

Faced with the closure of the port, Boston appealed to all the colonies for help. As a result representatives from all the colonies except Georgia met in the First Continental Congress at Philadelphia on 5 September 1774 to discuss opposition to British policy. The debates soon showed divided opinion. Some congress members wanted to retain political ties with Britain. Others wanted independence. The outcome was a set of compromise decisions: Britain's 'bullying' tactics were condemned and a boycott of British goods was organised. The Continental Congress is less important for its decisions than for the fact that it showed that many people wanted to break from Britain.

During the winter of 1774 and 1775 patriotic groups mustered arms and ammunition for a war that they thought inevitable. It was while British troops were hunting for arms that fighting began. From Boston, general Gage sent some soldiers to seize weapons at the village of Concord; they were also to arrest two patriot leaders there, Samuel Adams and John Hancock. The troops departed on 18 April 1775, but at Lexington, a village on the way, were met by a band of just over fifty colonists. Shooting broke out; the troops pushed on to Concord and destroyed what arms they could find. All the way back to Boston they were attacked by groups of colonists, and lost 247 men.

War fever swept through the colonies. Massachusetts formed an army; volunteers poured in from all sides. Everything now

Entitled 'Retreat of the British from Concord' this print shows British troops being attacked by colonists.

depended on the attitude of the British government and the Second Continental Congress that was called for May 1775.

So far as the British were concerned, they would give no concessions. In 1774 and 1775 Parliament petitioned George III to enforce his authority. In spite of the opposition from the colonists the British position was simple: the colonists must either submit, or Britain would force them to give in.

When the Second Continental Congress met again in Philadelphia, it still was undecided on what to do. It created an army and appointed George Washington as commander-in-chief of the New England troops; even so, some members still hoped to settle the differences with Britain. As the year passed, however, it became clear that British policy would not alter, and therefore after a long, complicated debate, the Congress decided upon independence. A committee of five, headed by Thomas Jefferson, prepared a Declaration of Independence that was adopted on 4 July 1776.

The Declaration of Independence stated, 'that all men are created equal, that they are endowed by their Creator with certain unalienable Rights, that among these are Life, Liberty and the pursuit of Happiness'. It went on that, 'whenever any Form of Government becomes destructive of these ends, it is the Right of the People to alter or to abolish it, and to institute new Government . . .' It further claimed that, 'the history of the present King of Great Britain is a history of repeated injuries and usurpations, all having in direct object the establishment of an absolute Tyranny over these States', and then listed the 'tyrannous' deeds of the king. The Declaration of Independence

concluded that because of the tyranny of British policy, 'these United Colonies are, and of Right ought to be Free and Independent States . . . Absolved from all Allegiance to the British Crown, and that all political connection between them and the State of Great Britain, is and ought to be dissolved'.

The Declaration of Independence was intended not only to explain the position of the colonies but also to win sympathy in Europe for their cause. The colonists hoped to gain military assistance in the inevitable struggle, for they understood that their chances of success without foreign help were small.

The War

War now began in earnest. At first the Americans fought alone, aided only by volunteers from Europe. When, however, they showed themselves capable of matching the British, especially when they forced a British army to surrender at Saratoga on 17 October 1777, several European states were ready to give aid. Alliances were signed with France (1778), Spain (1779) and Holland (1780), and it was the help given by these powers that decided the outcome of the war. Their fleets seriously hampered, and even cut off British communications with America. The French sent an army of 8,000 under Rochambeau to help the Americans. After a series of victories in 1780, this army in conjunction with an American army under Washington, forced the besieged British at Yorktown to surrender in October 1781. The victory virtually brought the war to an end. Peace negotiations opened, and terms were signed at Versailles in 1783. Britain recognised the independence of the United States of America and gave up to them all lands west of the line laid down by the Proclamation of 1763. These were generous terms,

The Declaration of Independence was adopted on 4 July 1776.

'We hold these truths to be self-evident, that all men are created equal, that they are endowed by their Creator with certain unalienable Rights, that among these are Life, Liberty and the pursuit of Happiness'.

The Declaration of Independence

12

The surrender of the British under General Cornwallis at Yorktown, October 1781.

but the British government hoped that concessions given in 1783 would secure influence with American governments in the future.

The Problem of Government

After the Declaration of Independence plans were needed for the future government of the states. A special committee was appointed to draw up a plan, and the scheme that this committee produced was called the 'Articles of Confederation'. The Articles reacted against strong central government. The committee wanted a loose federation of states with a weak central government which could not, for example, raise taxes, raise armed forces, or compel individual states to accept any of its laws with which they did not agree. When the war finished, the Articles were criticised for having left too many powers in the hands of individual states. A group called the Federalists argued this case, and collected much support for their view that a new constitution should be written, in which the central government would have far more authority than that provided by the Articles of Confederation. Some modern historians maintain that the Federalist criticisms were exaggerated, and that the Articles could have worked after some additions to the powers of the central government.

The Federalists had their way and in May 1787 a convention met at Philadelphia to draft a new constitution. George Washington presided, and other important figures included

We the People

of the United States, in Order to form a more perfect Union, establish Justice, insure domestic Tranquility, provide for the common defence, promote the general Welfare, and secure the Blessings of Liberty to ourselves and our Posterity, do ordain and establish this Constitution for the United States of America.

Article. I.

Section. 1. All legislative Powers herein granted shall be vested in a Congress of the United States, which shall consist of a Senate and House of Representatives.

Section. 2. The House of Representatives shall be composed of Members chosen every second Year by the People of the several States, and the Electors in each State shall have the Qualifications requisite for Electors of the most numerous Branch of the State Legislature.

No Person shall be a Representative who shall not have attained to the Age of twenty five Years, and been seven Years a Citizen of the United States, and who shall not, when elected, be an Inhabitant of that State in which he shall be chosen.

Representatives and direct Taxes shall be apportioned among the several States which may be included within this Union, according to their respective Numbers, which shall be determined by adding to the whole Number of free Persons, including those bound to Service for a Term of Years, and excluding Indians not taxed, three fifths of all other Persons. The actual Enumeration shall be made within three Years after the first Meeting of the Congress of the United States, and within every subsequent Term of ten Years, in such Manner as they shall by Law direct. The Number of Representatives shall not exceed one for every thirty Thousand, but each State shall have at Least one Representative; and until such enumeration shall be made, the State of New Hampshire shall be entitled to chuse three, Massachusetts eight, Rhode-Island and Providence Plantations one, Connecticut five, New-York six, New Jersey four, Pennsylvania eight, Delaware one, Maryland six, Virginia ten, North Carolina five, South Carolina five, and Georgia three.

When vacancies happen in the Representation from any State, the Executive Authority thereof shall issue Writs of Election to fill such Vacancies.

The House of Representatives shall chuse their Speaker and other Officers; and shall have the sole Power of Impeachment.

Section. 3. The Senate of the United States shall be composed of two Senators from each State, chosen by the Legislature thereof, for six Years; and each Senator shall have one Vote.

Immediately after they shall be assembled in Consequence of the first Election, they shall be divided as equally as may be into three Classes. The Seats of the Senators of the first Class shall be vacated at the Expiration of the second Year, of the second Class at the Expiration of the fourth Year, and of the third Class at the Expiration of the sixth Year, so that one third may be chosen every second Year; and if Vacancies happen by Resignation, or otherwise, during the Recess of the Legislature of any State, the Executive thereof may make temporary Appointments until the next Meeting of the Legislature, which shall then fill such Vacancies.

No Person shall be a Senator who shall not have attained to the Age of thirty Years, and been nine Years a Citizen of the United States, and who shall not, when elected, be an Inhabitant of that State for which he shall be chosen.

The Vice President of the United States shall be President of the Senate, but shall have no Vote, unless they be equally divided.

The Senate shall chuse their other Officers, and also a President pro tempore, in the Absence of the Vice President, or when he shall exercise the Office of President of the United States.

——————

The Senators and Representatives before mentioned, and the Members of the several State Legislatures, and all executive and judicial Officers, both of the United States and of the several States, shall be bound by Oath or Affirmation, to support this Constitution; but no religious Test shall ever be required as a Qualification to any Office or public Trust under the United States.

Article. VII.

The Ratification of the Conventions of nine States, shall be sufficient for the Establishment of this Constitution between the States so ratifying the Same.

The Word "the", being interlined between the seventh and eighth Lines of the first Page, The Word "Thirty" being partly written on an Erazure in the fifteenth Line of the first Page. The Word "is" being interlined between the thirty second and thirty third Lines of the first Page and the Word "the" being interlined between the forty third and forty fourth Lines of the second Page.

done in Convention by the Unanimous Consent of the States present the Seventeenth Day of September in the Year of our Lord one thousand seven hundred and Eighty seven and of the Independance of the United States of America the Twelfth. In Witness whereof We have hereunto subscribed our Names,

Attest William Jackson Secretary

G°. Washington—Presid.
and deputy from Virginia

Delaware
Geo: Read
Gunning Bedford jun
John Dickinson
Richard Bassett
Jaco: Broom

Maryland
James McHenry
Dan of St Thos. Jenifer
Danl Carroll

Virginia
John Blair—
James Madison Jr.

North Carolina
Wm. Blount
Richd. Dobbs Spaight.
Hu Williamson

South Carolina
J. Rutledge
Charles Cotesworth Pinckney
Charles Pinckney
Pierce Butler

Georgia
William Few
Abr Baldwin

New Hampshire
John Langdon
Nicholas Gilman

Massachusetts
Nathaniel Gorham
Rufus King

Connecticut
Wm. Saml. Johnson
Roger Sherman

New York
Alexander Hamilton

New Jersey
Wil: Livingston
David Brearley.
Wm. Paterson.
Jona: Dayton

Pennsylvania
B Franklin
Thomas Mifflin
Robt. Morris
Geo. Clymer
Thos. FitzSimons
Jared Ingersoll
James Wilson
Gouv Morris

George Washington (1732–99).
He fought for the British against
the French in America during the
Seven Years war and then became
a planter; after commanding the
American forces in the war of
independence he again retired,
but returned to public life to take
a leading part in overthrowing the
Articles of Confederation and in
forming the Constitution; he was
elected first president of the U.S.A.
in 1789, was re-elected in 1792,
but refused to stand for a third
term of office.

The first and last articles of the
Constitution of the United States
of America with the signatures of
the Founding Fathers.

Benjamin Franklin and Alexander Hamilton. The fifty-five
members of the convention completed their task by mid-
September 1787, and the new constitution was accepted by
all the states by early 1790.

The Constitution

The Constitution divided the central (Federal) government
into three parts. The first was the law-making or legislative
branch, Congress. It had two houses, the Senate (two Senators
per state) and the House of Representatives (the Representatives
were divided among the states according to population).

Second was the executive branch headed by the President.
The President's role was to put laws into effect, but he was also
head of the armed forces and responsible for foreign affairs.

Finally came the judicial branch, the Supreme Court, which
ensured that all laws obeyed the Constitution.

The central government had six main functions. It had to hold
the states together, make sure that justice was applied equally
throughout the states, keep peace in the states, form a united
defence against foreign aggressors, improve the standard of
living of American citizens, and protect their rights. In order to
simplify this last task, a Bill of Rights defining human liberties
was passed and came into force in 1791. It stressed freedom
of worship, the freedom of the press, the right to carry weapons,
freedom from unauthorised arrest, and trial by jury.

Beyond this, many powers were left in the hands of the individual states. Education, medical care, local communications,
police, regulations on business affairs and working conditions,
these and many other matters were left the responsibility of
the states.

A Comment

The American Revolution has been seen in many ways. Some
writers have seen it just as an anti-British movement; they have
said that if the British had been more tactful there would have
been no revolution. Others have said that a revolution was
bound to come sooner or later because of the growth of democracy in the colonies. The Declaration of Independence and the
Constitution both used democratic ideas about the freedom of
the individual and human rights; this is seen by some historians
as proof that the revolution was democratic in character. Yet
other historians see it as an economic struggle for the riches
of America. Whatever the most accurate interpretation, one
thing is sure; contemporary Europeans watched the American
Revolution, drew their own conclusions about it, and in many
cases wanted to apply American ideas to Europe.

Things to Do

1. Find out more about George Washington and Thomas Jefferson.
2. Examine the Declaration of Independence and the American Constitution (both can be found in the *Encyclopaedia Britannica*).
3. Make out a case on behalf of the British and then on behalf of the Americans.
4. Read about the war for independence; why did the Americans win?

Books to Read or Consult

J. R. Alden, *The American Revolution, 1775-83,* London 1954.

J. ter Haar, *The Story of America,* London 1967.

J. C. Miller, *Origins of the American Revolution,* Oxford 1966.

H. Rankin, *The American Revolution,* London 1964.

M. Rivoire, *The Life and Times of Washington,* London 1967.

The Forces of Change in Europe

Introduction

Although European society looked reasonably stable in the eighteenth century, from about 1770 onwards there was growing social, political, and economic disorder. The reasons for this are often found by studying individual countries, but there were also general forces at work that combined to produce turmoil throughout most of the continent.

The Growth of Population

One general trend was the growth of the European population. In 1700 it was about 118 millions, but by 1800 it had risen to

A peasant farm labourer.

he French agricultural system was ncapable of producing enough ood.

Agriculture, Labourage.

17

The middle classes, including lawyers as shown here, grew in numbers and wealth.

190 millions. France is typical of this development, for while her population stood at about 20 millions in 1700, it reached 28 millions by 1800.

The expanding population created problems, above all in France. Somehow the ever-increasing millions had to be fed, but the French agricultural system was incapable of producing enough food, especially at times of bad harvests such as occurred in the 1780s. Again, employment had to be found for the growing population, but since there was little industry to employ large numbers of people there never was enough work available. As a result, by 1789 unemployment was one of the most serious social problems in France. Difficulties such as these led to widespread discontent which made an important contribution to the French Revolution.

A peasant sets off with his family to celebrate a public holiday.

Descartes (1596–1650).

Voltaire (1694–1778).

Social Changes

The growth of the European population was accompanied by changes in society. For one thing the middle classes (merchants, bankers, lawyers, doctors, civil servants, teachers and shop owners) grew in numbers and wealth. They were stronger in western Europe than in eastern Europe, for most large towns were in the west. Furthermore, the west European ports enjoyed a flourishing Atlantic trade which contributed to the prosperity of the towns, and therefore of the middle classes who dwelt there.

Although the middle classes were generally well-off financially, in parts of Germany and in France they had a serious grievance; they did not have enough political power. They wanted more positions in local and central government so that their political importance in society would equal their economic importance.

Changes also took place among the peasants of Europe. By the middle of the eighteenth century feudalism had died out in Britain, the Netherlands and northern Italy. It still survived, though to varying degrees, in Germany and France, where the peasants had a strong desire to abolish feudalism and own the land which they cultivated.

The Enlightenment

As well as social changes, eighteenth century Europe produced the Enlightenment. This was an intellectual movement that examined the whole of eighteenth century European civilisation, pointed out its weaknesses, and suggested ways of improvement.

19

ENCYCLOPÉDIE,
OU
DICTIONNAIRE RAISONNÉ
DES SCIENCES,
DES ARTS ET DES MÉTIERS,
PAR UNE SOCIÉTÉ DE GENS DE LETTRES.
MIS EN ORDRE ET PUBLIÉ PAR M². ***.

Tantùm feries junɛturaque pollet,
Tantùm de medio fumptis accedit honoris! HORAT.

TOME NEUVIEME.

JU = MAM

A GENEVE,
CHEZ CRAMER L'AINÉ & Compagnie.

M. DCC. LXXII.

Title page of the ninth volume of the *Encyclopaedia.*

The *philosophes* (as the writers of the Enlightenment are called) followed certain methods when they studied and commented upon society. One was the scientific approach. They observed society as a scientist might observe an experiment, and tried to discover why injustices existed. Voltaire (1694–1778) did this in his *Letters on the English* (1735). He was in England from 1726 to 1728, and he considered it a much freer country than his native France. As a result of his observations, he concluded that it was religious toleration, the principle that

20

ontesquieu (1689–1755).

everybody is equal before the law, and the guarantee of the liberty of the individual and his property, that made England preferable to France.

The other main approach was that of the seventeenth century French mathematician and philosopher, Descartes (1596–1650). He had argued that man's greatest gift is his ability to reason or think logically, and in his *Discourse on Method* (1637) he outlined his system of thinking. Many eighteenth century *philosophes* followed his method and considered how far European society was built on rational foundations, and in what ways it needed to be changed. Montesquieu (1689–1755) took this approach. He studied the laws in different countries, and tried to sort out those that were most just; he hoped that these would form the basis of a fairer legal system in France and elsewhere. This was the theme of *The Spirit of the Laws* (1748), a work in which he maintained that the most rational, and thus the most just, system of government is one where the law-making body (the legislature), the law-enforcing body (the executive), and the law-preserving body (the judiciary) are separate from each other. This idea was accepted by the American Constitution.

iderot, co-editor of the ncyclopaedia.

The *philosophes* in the different countries of Europe suggested means of reforming almost every aspect of life. They proposed legal reforms, political reforms, religious reforms, educational reforms, economic reforms, and expressed their ideas through pamphlets, letters, novels and discussion groups. By far their greatest achievement and instrument of publicity, however, was the *Encyclopaedia;* it was made up of seventeen volumes and was published between 1751 and 1772. Its editors were Diderot and d'Alembert, and the articles in it were written by *philosophes* such as Rousseau (author of *The Social Contract*), Voltaire and Montesquieu. The articles were used to criticise existing society and to outline reforms; the *Encyclopaedia*, in fact, mapped out a new European society.

The Political Struggle

In the second half of the eighteenth century a struggle took place between monarchs and the aristocracy (both lay and clerical). It was a conflict over money and political power.

After the war of the Austrian Succession and the Seven Years war, every monarch in Europe was short of cash. The English government tried to solve the problem by imposing more taxes on the colonies; on the continent, many monarchs taxed the aristocracy. This was a startling move, since in most countries the aristocracy was traditionally free from most (although not all) taxes. The nobles resisted, and so monarchs had to break their political power before the taxes could be imposed effectively.

This was no easy task, for the aristocracy in many countries enjoyed immense political authority. In Hungary, Poland and Sweden they dominated the diets. In Prussia they controlled most of the provincial diets. In Switzerland they dominated the cantons.

Parliament

In France the struggle between Louis XVI and the nobles ended in apparent victory for the latter. In 1775 Turgot, Louis' leading minister, produced a plan for a new system of taxation, and the principal tax was to be a land tax upon all ranks of society. He believed that this was the only way of setting the French government on a firm financial footing. He was bitterly attacked by the aristocracy, who saw the plan as an attack upon their rights and privileges, and a way of turning the king into an all-powerful monarch whose authority they would not be able to check. So widespread was opposition that Louis gave in and dismissed Turgot in 1776.

This was not the end of the story. Turgot's successors failed to solve the government's financial problems, which grew worse and worse and needed drastic remedies. The government's income through taxation was consistently less than its expenses; the deficit in the 1780s was to the tune of about 70 to 80 million francs a year. French involvement in the American Revolution cost 2,000 million francs, and the government had to borrow vast amounts of money at a high rate of interest to meet the cost. Year by year the debts rose and no means was found of paying them off.

By 1786, Calonne, who was then leading minister, decided that there was only one solution; to accept Turgot's scheme of 1775 for a completely new approach to taxation.

It was obvious to Calonne that if Turgot's plan were reintroduced, then the aristocratic opposition that had broken out in 1775 would also appear. He therefore searched for means of reforming taxation without being foiled by the aristocracy. In fact there was no way. The Assembly of Notables, a hand-picked aristocratic body that Louis called in the hope that its members (chosen for their royalist sympathies) would accept reform, refused to do so. Its opposition in 1787 was repeated all over the country; the *parlements* (these were law courts, many of whose members were aristocrats) denounced the proposed tax reforms as despotic, and demanded that an Estates General be called to discuss the problems between king and subjects. The aristocracy everywhere attacked the suggested reforms, and welcomed the idea of an Estates General at which they would be represented, and where they could express their

d'Alembert, co-editor of the *Encyclopaedia*.

Rousseau, author of *The Social Contract*.

Fashionable young man and women of late eighteenth century Paris.

objections to the king's policies. Louis agreed, and an Estates General was planned for 1789.

The example of France is particularly important because the conflict between Louis XVI and the aristocracy was to let loose full scale revolution by the lower classes of society. This revolution forced the king and the aristocracy into alliance.

The Example of the American Revolution

To everybody in Europe who wanted to change society, the American Revolution and the establishment of a republic based upon a written constitution, were a powerful source of encouragement. America was closely studied in the press, the learned societies and the smart intellectual *salons*. Admiration for the new republic was encouraged by European soldiers who had fought for the Americans against the British, and many, such as La Fayette the Frenchman, wanted to see their own countries reformed on the American model.

It was in the 1780s, indeed, that America first became the dream of many Europeans. Americans lived in a republic, but most Europeans were governed by kings; Americans had a Bill of Rights, but most Europeans had very few rights; America appeared a land of liberty, while Europe seemed to deny liberty to most people. This dream was too simple, for America was not the land of universal liberty that Europeans thought. This does not matter. Europeans believed the dream, and hoped to make it come true in their own countries. In the numerous revolutions that occurred in Europe at the end of the eighteenth

Turgot (1727–81), Louis XVI's leading minister (1774–6).

23

century, there were deliberate attempts by revolutionaries to imitate the American style of revolution, and the creation of a constitution.

It was not long after the American Revolution before revolution broke out in Europe. In the 1780s it occurred in the Dutch Republic, the Habsburg empire, Switzerland and France. It was the French Revolution that was to be the most serious and that was to have the widest effect on Europe. To that revolution we can now turn.

Things to Do

1. Study the lives of Voltaire, Montesquieu and Rousseau; try to find copies of some of their writings.
2. Read about one of the Enlightened Despots such as Frederick II of Prussia or Joseph II of Austria. Compare their problems with those of Louis XVI, and compare their handling of the problems with his.
3. Study the French aristocracy. Do you think that they opposed Louis XVI for purely selfish reasons, or had they a case for doing so?

Books to Read or Consult

C. B. A. Behrens, *The Ancien Regime,* London 1967.

A. B. C. Cobban, *A History of Modern France,* vol. 1, London 1965.

A. Goodwin, *The European Nobility in the Eighteenth Century,* 1967.

G. Lefèbvre, *The Coming of the French Revolution,* Oxford 1968.

Louis XVI.

24

The French Revolution

Emmanuel Joseph Sieyès (1748–1836). A canon of Chartres cathedral (usually known as Abbé Sieyès), he represented Paris at the Estates General; during the 1790's he was cautious and wary of making enemies; he became a Director in 1799, and enlisted Napoleon's help in overthrowing the Directory; Napoleon later ousted him from power, and under the empire he was given no offices; he lived in exile from 1815–30.

The Estates General: the Background

Some of the major difficulties of France were mentioned in the previous chapter. The Estates General of 1789 was intended to deal with them. The Estates General was not a regular body and had not met since 1614. It was elected and had the right to discuss and take decisions upon national affairs. It was divided into three Orders or sections: the Clergy (308 members in 1789), the Aristocracy (285 members), and the Third Estate (621 members). It was opened at Versailles by Louis XVI on 5 May.

The trouble was that the king and the Orders had different aims in the Estates General. The king wanted reforms of the taxation system. He knew that the Clergy and the Aristocracy would oppose him; therefore he must win the support of the Third Estate to back him up.

Most, although not all, of the Clergy and Aristocracy were determined to protect their rights and privileges; in other words they were opposed to reforms. To this end they hoped to form an alliance with the Third Estate against the king.

The Third Estate was thus in the happy position that the king on one side, and the Clergy and Aristocracy on the other, wanted its support. Almost all the members of the Third Estate were from the middle classes. They believed strongly in the ideals of the Enlightenment, and therefore wanted reforms, not only of taxation, but of almost every aspect of society. During the winter of 1788–9 members of the middle classes had published large numbers of pamphlets in preparation for the Estates General. The most famous was by the Abbé Sieyès, and was entitled, *What is the Third Estate?* In this pamphlet he urged the middle classes to play a much fuller part in the political life of the state. The aims of the Third Estate were further formed by *cahiers*. These were lists of grievances drawn up by various bodies in the provinces for presentation at the Estates General. They called for changes in such practical matters as taxation and clerical and aristocratic privilege. Aristocrats (a class which included bishops) were exempt from many taxes, especially the *taille* (the principal tax). They still could demand feudal dues from peasants (although in the eighteenth century this was done in only a few parts of the country); the Church also could collect special taxes from the peasants. The outcome was that the Third Estate appeared at Versailles determined not to be the instrument of the king or of the two other Orders, but with a programme of its own.

25

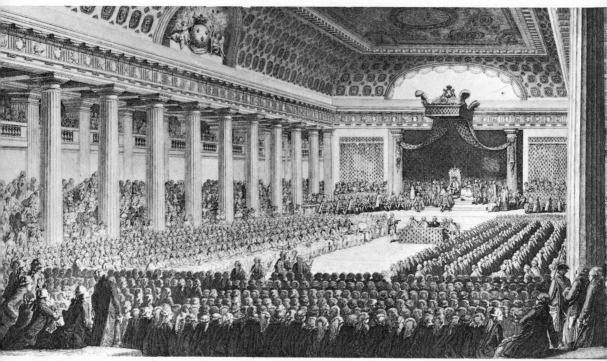

Opening of the Estates General 5 May 1789.

The Estates General Fails: the National Assembly Takes Over

The Estates General met amid much optimism. There was great expectation that France's problems were soon to be solved. The first question to be discussed concerned the system of voting in the Estates General. The Third Estate wanted one vote per member, so that its 621 delegates could outvote the two remaining Orders. The Clergy and Aristocracy wanted one vote per Order, so that together they could outvote the Third Estate.

The issue was debated for almost six weeks without decision. The enthusiasm of the early days turned to frustration, and at last the Third Estate staged a mass walk-out on 17 June. Not only that: it took the startling step of adopting the title 'National Assembly', which implied that it alone represented the nation. N.B. Three days later the members hardened their position by taking an oath not to disband until a new constitution had been written. This was an act of open revolution.

During the next few days Louis could not decide what to do. His mind was made up for him. The Clergy and Aristocracy were not so united as they appeared. About half of the clergy and twenty per cent of the Aristocracy voluntarily joined the National Assembly. Louis gave in and on 27 June commanded

26

A *cahier* or list of grievances prepared for presentation at the Estates General.

the rest of the Clergy and Aristocracy to join the National Assembly. The Estates General was dead: the National Assembly was in control.

The Growth of Public Opinion

Events in the Estates General and later in the National Assembly were followed by the public with immense interest. Large numbers of pamphlets appeared attacking the *ancien régime* and whipping up public demand for reform. The traveller Arthur Young, who was in France in 1789, wrote that, 'Nineteen-

twentieths of these productions are in favour of liberty, and commonly violent against the clergy and nobility'.

The 'Great Fear' and the Fall of the Bastille

Hatred of the *ancien régime* turned to panic when rumours spread that the king was planning to overthrow the National Assembly. In July he called 20,000 troops to Paris, and the frightened population thought that an attack was coming. Rioting broke out and reached a climax on 14 July. The crowds wanted arms and ammunition. They seized weapons and then

The members of the National Assembly, who had met in a tennis court, took an oath not to disband until a new constitution had been written. This is known as the Tennis Court oath.

The taking of the Bastille, 14 July 1789.

28

marched on the Bastille, where there was said to be a vast store of ammunition. The Bastille was the most famous prison in France, and was a symbol of the oppression of the *ancien régime*. After an assault lasting four hours, the Bastille fell, an event taken as a triumph for the people and a death-blow to the *ancien régime*. Edward Rigby, an English physician in Paris at this time, described the joy of the crowds thus:

A sudden burst of the most frantic joy . . . took place. Shouts and shrieks, leaping and embracing, laughter and tears, every sound and every gesture, manifested, among the . . . crowd, such an instantaneous and unanimous emotion of extreme gladness as I should suppose was never before experienced by human beings.

From this point on the French Revolution was not just the concern of the National Assembly, but actively involved the masses in the towns.

The French peasants regarded the nobility and clergy as burdens as shown in this picture where a peasant carries a nobleman and clergyman on his back.

The Peasant Revolution

Revolution struck the countryside too. The peasants turned on the aristocrats. They refused to pay their feudal dues, they

With the title 'Hunting Aristocrats' this print illustrates the fear which aristocrats had for their lives and why they fled the country.

29

The Declaration of the Rights of Man.

burnt documents listing their duties, and even looted some of the châteaux. Their anger turned to terror when stories spread that furious noblemen had hired gangs of robbers to attack the peasants. Nobody knew what was happening; everybody lived in fear. Aristocrats were now afraid for their lives and began to flee. By the middle of September 1789 over 200,000 had left the country, certain that the old France was gone for ever.

The rising of the peasants alarmed the National Assembly. In an attempt to quieten the countryside, it announced in

Adieu Bastille: the privileged orders are shown as puppets performing to the tune of the Third Estate.

Honoré Gabriel de Riquetti, comte de Mirabeau (1749–91). An aristocrat who supported reform in France; he passed an erratic youth, during which he spent several terms in prison; he sat in the Estates General as a member of the Third Estate, and shone as an outstanding orator; he was suspicious of extremists and in the Constitution of 1791 supported the idea of a royal veto; in 1791 he became president of the Constituent Assembly, but died in office.

August the abolition of feudalism. This decree succeeded in reducing the violence of the peasant rising.

The Declaration of the Rights of Man

Meanwhile, on 9 July, the National Assembly took the title 'Constituent Assembly', and set about writing a constitution. It drew upon ideas expressed in the Enlightenment, and followed the American example by producing a Declaration of the Rights of Man and the Citizen. The rights were defined thus: all men are born equal before the law; they should enjoy freedom of religion, of speech, and of the press; they should be able to own property in safety: the state exists to protect these rights and should be governed by representatives of citizens, for sovereignty belongs to the citizens, not to a monarch.

The Declaration set the principles which the Constitution was to follow. Outside of France it was hailed as a victory for liberty. The freedom that the U.S.A. had won seemed to have arrived in France.

The Constitution

The Constituent Assembly worked for two years, and in 1791 produced the Constitution:

Political Change

The position of the king was altered. He had to obey the Constitution and could no longer make laws; this was to be done by a Legislative Assembly. The Assembly was to be elected by people who paid a certain amount in taxes; the Assembly

31

Usage des Nouvelles Mesures.

1. le Litre (*Pour la* Pinte)
2. le Gramme (*Pour la* Livre)
3. le Mètre (*Pour l'*Aune)
4. l'Are (*Pour la* Toise)
5. le Franc(*Pour une* Livre Tournois)
6. le Stere (*Pour la* Denne Voie de Bois)

Déposé à la Bibᵗʰᵉ Nˡᵉ le 24 Ventose An 8. | *A Paris chez Delion Rue Montmartre Nᵒ 242 pres le Boulevard*

J.P Delion G..... inv.   Labrousse Sculp

The use of the new metric measures which were introduced at this time.

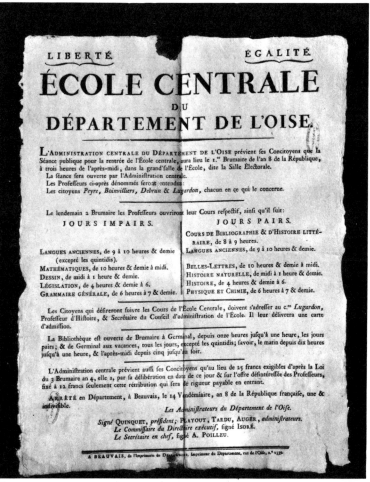

The programme for an *École
centrale* in 1799.

thus represented mainly the middle classes. The king could veto its laws, but must accept them if the Assembly insisted.

Administrative and Legal Change

The Constituent Assembly wanted to abandon centralised administration, and give the people more say in local government. The country was divided into eighty-three Departments, which were subdivided into Districts and Cantons. They were all to be run by elected councils.

The legal system was brought into line with the administrative system. The Departments and Districts were to have their own courts, while in the Cantons, Justices of the Peace would deal with petty crime. In addition, judges would be elected and the jury system was adopted; these two measures were intended to give the people more influence in the application of the law.

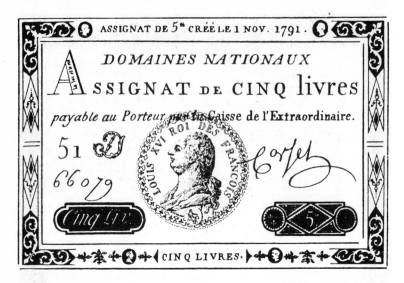

An *assignat*.

The Church

Most members of the Constituent Assembly were Catholics, and wanted to bring the Revolution and the Catholic Church together. They tried to do so through the Civil Constitution of the Clergy.

The boundaries of dioceses were made the same as those of the Departments, and those of parishes the same as the boundaries of the Districts. Bishops and priests were to be elected by special committees of the Departments and Districts, and all the clergy had to take an oath of loyalty to the state.

The clergy were deeply divided in their response to the Constitution, but wanted to know the pope's reaction. Pius VI hesitated for eight months, but in March 1791 condemned it. He was too late. By then almost half of the French clergy had sworn loyalty to the state, and the pope's decision simply made the split in the Catholic Church more serious.

Taxation

France was still faced with the financial weaknesses that had been so desperate in the 1770s and 1780s. The Constituent Assembly thought that it had the answers. Henceforth there would be three principal taxes, a land tax, a tax on property, and a tax upon the profits of commerce and industry. Nobody was to escape these taxes, but they would be proportional to a person's income. The scheme looked fine on paper, but no effective means of collecting the taxes was ever found.

The problem of paying off the state's debts was to be solved by seizing and selling Church property. This would be a long process, however, and the state needed cash quickly. Therefore

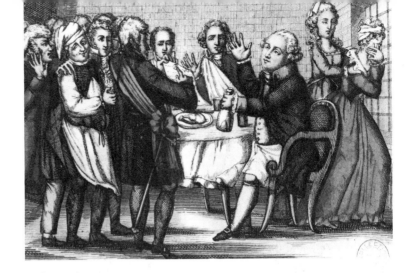

The arrest of the king at Varennes.

it was announced that people could pay money to the state immediately and receive special receipts (*assignats*), which could later be used to buy Church property. The plan began well, but people used the *assignats* as ordinary money, a practice so common that in 1790 the Constituent Assembly recognised them as such. This was disastrous. There was now more money in circulation, but shopkeepers, grainmerchants and other business men let food and other items onto the market only slowly; they demanded higher and higher prices as more and more money circulated. In other words more money in circulation equalled higher prices; money was worth less and less. This process (inflation) hit the poor severely.

France under the Constitution

On 30 September 1791 the Constituent Assembly disbanded and the Constitution was put into effect. The newly elected Legislative Assembly took over on 1 October. Although there were no political parties in the Assembly, there were certain recognisable groups. There were the Jacobins; republicans led by Robespierre and Marat. A more moderate group was known as the Girondins; led by Brissot, most of them were middle class and came from the south-west. Again, there were the Feuillants, a more conservative group led by La Fayette and Barnave. The remaining deputies can be classed under no heading; they adopted a moderate political outlook.

The Coming of War

To go back a little, in June 1791, Louis XVI in despair tried to escape from France. He was captured at Varennes and brought back to Paris. He appealed for help to the Austrian emperor, Leopold II. Leopold wanted to aid him but could get no active support from other governments. In August 1791, he and

The return of the king and of the royal family to Paris. The people greeted him with silence and did not remove their hats.

Frederick William II of Prussia announced the Declaration of Pillnitz, that called on monarchs to help Louis XVI if necessary.

Within the Constituent Assembly there was indignation. The Girondins wanted to declare war on Austria, but their view was opposed by Robespierre. He argued that war would destroy the ideals of the Revolution, and further maintained that the French army was unfit to fight. The call for war was taken up by the king's supporters, who hoped that in a war France would be beaten, the Austrians would invade, and Louis XVI would be restored to his authority.

The elections for the Legislative Assembly brought to it a majority of pro-war members. The turning-point came with the death of Leopold II on 1 March 1792. His successor, Francis II, detested the French Revolution. When the Legislative Assembly sent him a demand that he renounce the Declaration of Pillnitz, he refused. In April 1792 France therefore declared war on Austria.

Maximilien Marie Isidore de Robespierre (1758–94). A member of the Estates General, the Jacobin club and the Convention; a radical who dominated the Committee of Public Safety from 1793–4; historians once saw him simply as 'the monster' of the Terror, but now tend to be more sympathetic towards him; he was an idealist, he was honest and stood by his principles, although by doing so he kept the Terror going.

The War and its Effects on the Revolution

When the fighting began it soon became clear that Robespierre's fears about the weakness of French armies were justified. There was a mutiny among French troops on the northern frontier, and many deserted to the Austrians. Prussia joined in the war, and in July 1792 a Prussian army invaded France, accompanied by French aristocrats returning to wreak vengeance.

Faced with crisis, the Legislative Assembly in May recruited men for the National Guard, a volunteer army that would defend Paris and allow regular troops to go and fight the Austrians and Prussians. Louis chose this moment to step in. He vetoed the order, hoping to keep the armies on the frontier weak. Louis

On 10 August 1792 the king and family had to flee from a violent mob.

now stood in his true colours, a direct opponent of the Revolution. Public hostility towards him grew when at the end of July a message came from the Prussians saying that they intended restoring Louis to his rightful position, and that if he were harmed Paris would be heavily punished. Demonstrations and demands for his overthrow spread dramatically. So violent were they that on 10 August the king and his family had to flee from a mob, and take refuge with the Legislative Assembly. The chances of monarchy surviving in France now looked slim.

Meanwhile the Legislative Assembly had bypassed Louis' veto, and on 11 July issued the declaration, 'the Fatherland is in danger', which called for volunteers to join the National Guard. The Assembly also suspended the king, and agreed to the election of a National Convention that would review the Constitution and if necessary write a new one. This was a confession that the Constitution of 1791 could not work amidst crisis.

The National Convention and the Death of the King

Elections were held in September 1792 against a background of chaos. The Prussians seized Longwy and Verdun; in the west and south-west riots broke out in support of the king; in Paris there was panic again, and between 2 and 6 September a pointless, unorganised massacre took place of about 1,400 'enemies of the Revolution'.

As for the election, although universal suffrage was adopted, only about ten per cent of the electorate turned out. The Girondins won a majority, and the first act of the Convention, on 21 September, was to abolish the monarchy and declare a republic. It was also decided to try the king, but nobody knew what procedure to follow. A long debate resulted that dragged on until Christmas. At last a special commission was set up to prepare a list of the king's 'crimes'. The Convention discussed the 'crimes', found Louis guilty, and by a narrow majority voted for his death. Louis was executed on 21 January 1793.

The crowd tears down the statue of Louis XIV in the *Place des Victoires*, 11 August 1792.

The Girondins in Power

The war had by now taken a turn for the better. The Prussians had been expelled, and French troops had invaded the Austrian

The execution of Louis XVI, 21 January 1793.

Between 2 and 6 September the massacre of about 1400 'enemies the Revolution' took place.

Marie Antoinette (1755–93). An Austrian princess and wife of Louis XVI; she interfered in government, urged Louis XVI to resist the Revolution, and was popularly seen as a sinister influence on the king; she was executed by the revolutionaries in October 1793.

Netherlands, Savoy, Nice, and had crossed the Rhine. Flushed with success, the Convention in November 1792 offered aid to any European people that revolted against its rulers. It followed this up with the annexation of the conquered territories. These decisions, to which was added the execution of the king, created horror abroad. In 1793 Britain, Holland, Spain and many Italian states, joined Austria and Prussia in the war against France.

Worse was to follow. Dumouriez, France's most important general, deserted to the Austrians as La Fayette had done in autumn 1792. Riots broke out in Paris against the food shortage and rising prices. The civil war continued in the west and south-west.

In the Convention, the Jacobins led by Robespierre, Danton and Marat, attacked the bungling of the Girondins. They also won the support of the Parisian masses by demanding more food and the control of prices. The only important measures that the Girondins took were political; they organised bodies such as the Committee of Public Safety, whose purpose was to root out political suspects.

The Jacobins became convinced that the only way to save France from chaos at home and invasion from abroad, was to overthrow the Girondins. They schemed with the leaders of the 'Sections' into which Paris had been divided, and the plot was carried out on 2 June 1793. On that day the Section leaders presented a demand to the Convention for the arrest of the chief Girondins. They were supported by the National Guard and by the Jacobins inside the Convention. The Convention had to agree and twenty-nine prominent Girondins were arrested. This left the Jacobins in control.

The Jacobins in Power and the Terror

There was clearly a need for a period of strong government to bring the country under control and to organise the war effort.

This the Jacobins provided. They were helped by the Terror of 1793–4 which removed many possible opponents. On 13 July 1793, Marat was stabbed to death by Charlotte Corday, a supporter of the Girondins. Republican extremists saw this as symbolic of the Girondin threat to the Revolution. All over the country revolutionary committees (oddly enough created by the Girondins themselves) arrested, tried and executed 'counter-revolutionaries'. The Terror lasted until July 1794, and it is thought that about 400,000 people were arrested and 40,000 executed.

Meanwhile the Jacobins turned to the problem of governing France. Headed by Robespierre, Danton, and Carnot, they ruled through the small Committee of Public Safety, which had only twelve members, rather than through the cumbersome Convention. Strict measures were taken. The civil war in the west and south-west had spread to the south, but was put down by the use of regular troops; the Terror effectively mopped up the remaining opponents of the Jacobins there. In order to conduct the war more efficiently a call-up of all men between the ages of eighteen and twenty-five was announced. As a result French armies numbered almost one million men. The economy was put on a war footing, so that the textiles industry, for example, was turned to the production of war goods. To try and check inflation, the Jacobins imposed a maximum beyond which wages and prices were not to rise.

It was this last decision that contributed to their undoing. Although wages were fixed, prices continued to mount. This created widespread discontent, especially among the Parisian masses upon whose support the Jacobins heavily relied. In

Georges Jacques Danton (1759–94). He started out as an extremist in the Revolution but gradually became more moderate; he was extremely popular with the Parisian masses, and the overthrow of the monarchy was mainly his doing; as a leading member of the Committee of Public Safety his two chief aims were to pursue the war and settle peace at home; he tried to restrain the extremism of Robespierre, but was arrested and executed.

ean Paul Marat (1744–93).
Born in Switzerland he was court
physician in France from 1777 to
1786; he became an ardent
Jacobin and was bitterly anti-
royalist; in 1792 he became a
member of the Convention,
and took a prominent part in
instigating the September
massacres; widely hated, few
people mourned his death by
assassination.

spring 1794 the Committee of Public Safety ordered the seizure
of the property of 'traitors', and denied legal aid to suspects
when they were tried by revolutionary committees. These two
acts cut across the Declaration of the Rights of Man, and therefore across the principles of the original Revolution; moderate
opinion throughout the country was shocked. What is more,
the Committee of Public Safety was itself divided. By June
1794 Robespierre, who now wanted to end the Terror, was
quarrelling with other members of the Committee who wanted
to continue it. In the Convention he was criticised for his
handling of the war. Robespierre decided that he must protect
himself by removing his opponents. On 26 July he appeared at
the Convention and made a speech denouncing his enemies.
His critics in the Convention feared that he was preparing
them for the guillotine, and so decided to strike first. On 27
July in the Convention, Louchet proposed Robespierre's arrest;
amid tumult the Convention agreed. Robespierre was taken
prisoner later that day, quickly tried, and executed on 28 July
with twenty-one supporters.

The Moderates Take Over

Now that Robespierre had gone, moderates in the Convention
took measures to end the Jacobin rule. Jacobin clubs were
closed, the Terror was halted, and the maximum on wages and
prices abolished.

The Convention still had its original task of 1792 to perform,
namely to write a new constitution. In 1793 it had produced a
scheme which would have made the Constitution of 1791 more

The arrest of Robespierre,
27 July 1794.

democratic, but because of the war it was not introduced. In any case, there were two factors that convinced the Convention that the plan of 1793 would not work. One was the experience of the Terror, which persuaded moderates that the masses were incapable of acting in a responsible political manner, and must therefore be excluded from political affairs. The other was the Jacobin dictatorship, which taught the lesson that a small group of men should not be able to control government. The Convention therefore wrote another constitution which appeared in 1795.

The Constitution of 1795

In this constitution the Legislative Assembly was split into two Councils; the Council of Ancients (250 deputies) and the Council of Five Hundred. Each year one third of the members of the Councils were to be elected under a system of voting which still imposed tax qualifications, although they were less severe than in 1791.

The executive authority was also divided, this time between five Directors, known collectively as the Directory. They would be chosen by the Council of Ancients from a list prepared by the Council of Five Hundred. Each year one Director was to be replaced.

The administrative system remained similar to that of 1791. The Districts were abolished, and the Departments were to be run by elected councils of five men plus a representative of the Directory.

La Femme du Sans Culotte

In October 1795 the Convention disbanded; in November the Directory took over. The two most influential Directors were Barras and Carnot.

The Directory

The Directory did not enjoy complete control of the country. In May 1796 there was an unsuccessful attempt by a group of republican extremists to overthrow the Directory. More serious still was the growth of royalism. *Émigrés* began to return. Aided secretly by funds from Britain they formed groups such as the Friends of Order. Their purpose was to support royalist candidates in elections, win control of the two Councils, and legally bring back the monarchy. The strength of the movement was seen in the 1797 election which returned a majority of royalists.

As if this was not bad enough, economic difficulties continued. The removal of the maximum had led to an upsurge in prices. *Assignats* were still being produced, and their value was still declining; when the Directory came to power the 100 francs *assignat* was in fact worth only about 15 francs.

A conflict arose between the Directory and the Councils. The issue was the war. The Directory wanted to continue fighting, while the two Councils wanted peace. The moderates in the Councils now saw war as a threat to their control of the Revolution, while the royalists saw it as a hindrance to their plans.

Even the Directory itself showed signs of division. In 1797 a royalist, Barthélemy, joined the Directory, and found some support from Carnot.

In summer 1797, a group of royalists led by André (a member of the Council of Five Hundred) and Pichegru (president of the Council of Five Hundred) plotted against the Directory. In this dangerous position, the Directory appealed for help to Napoleon Bonaparte, who was leading a victorious French army on a campaign in Italy. He sent troops to Paris in support of the Directory, which was thus able to organise a counter-blow. In September 1797 royalist leaders were arrested, and 198 royalist deputies expelled from the Councils. The Directory was saved, but only because of the aid given by Napoleon Bonaparte.

Even now it was not fully safe. In 1798 war broke out again on a large scale. In an attempt to strike at Britain's links with India, and as part of a probable plan to create a French empire in the Middle East, Napoleon invaded Egypt. Although he successfully subjected it, his army was cut off from France when a British fleet under Nelson destroyed Napoleon's fleet at Aboukir Bay. Meanwhile in Europe a new anti-French

The *sans culottes* were the working class republicans in Paris during the Revolution; they were so called because they wore trousers instead of breeches ('sans culotte' = 'without breeches').

coalition, whose most important members were Britain, Russia, and Austria, had been formed and was waging war on France.

Within France itself the Directory was once again subject to opposition. After the expulsion of royalists from the Councils, Jacobins had returned, and were demanding the restoration of the Committee of Public Safety now that France was under the threat of invasion. Royalist uprisings broke out in the west and south-west.

When Napoleon heard this news he abandoned his army in Egypt, and returned to France in October 1799, full of plans to save the country from internal and external threats. The Abbé Sieyès, one of the Directors, persuaded Napoleon that the only answer was to abolish the Directory system and replace it with one in which the executive authority would be all-powerful, and the legislative authority weak. Another Director, Ducos, was brought into the plan, and together they decided upon a *coup*.

It came on 10 November 1799. On that day Napoleon, backed by troops, broke up the Council of Five Hundred. That evening some of the members of the Council gave consent to what was a fact; Sieyès, Napoleon and Ducos must write a new constitution. And so the end of the century saw yet another failure on the part of the French to produce a form of government that could both embody the principles of the Revolution and meet the immense problems of the day.

Napoleon Bonaparte.

Things to Do

1. Study the condition of the peasants on the eve of the Revolution.
2. Read about Louis XVI; how much responsibility must he bear for the outbreak of the Revolution?
3. Compare the French Constitution of 1791 with the American Constitution.
4. Imagine yourself in Paris during the revolution; compose a diary for the years 1793–5.
5. Study the life of Robespierre. Was he a monster or a genuine supporter of the Revolution?

Books to Read or Consult

D. L. Dowd, *The French Revolution,* London 1966.

A. Goodwin, *The French Revolution,* London 1966.

G. Salvemini, *The French Revolution, 1788-92,* London 1954.

J. M. Thompson, *The French Revolution,* London 1953.

France and Europe under Napoleon

Napoleon

1799 saw Napoleon's triumphant entry into French politics. What sort of a person was he? His outstanding quality was ambition, and this is the clue to understanding his character and career. It was ambition that drove him to control France and later Europe. He was never satisfied with his existing achievements, but must always press on to some new conquest. In his political thinking he was a product of the Enlightenment rather than of the Revolution. He had read widely among the works of the *philosophes*, especially Montesquieu and Voltaire. Like the *philosophes* he supported enlightened reforms, and believed that they could most effectively be introduced by an Enlightened Despot. When in power he saw himself as an Enlightened Despot rather than as a champion of the Revolution. Indeed, he was unsympathetic towards certain basic principles of the

apoleon Bonaparte in 1808.

French troops, under Napoleon, crossing the Alps.

Revolution; he scorned, for example, the idea of the sovereignty of the people.

His Rise to Power

Napoleon was born in Corsica in 1769 and was legally a Frenchman, since in 1768 France had bought Corsica from Genoa. At the age of nine he was sent to school in France, and in 1784 went to the famous Military School in Paris. After a year there he went into the army, and was stationed in France during the dramatic events of June and July 1789. In September he

Josephine de Beauharnais.

46

Napoleon as Emperor.

returned to Corsica where he spent most of his time until 1792; then he returned to France.

In France there was chaos, and it was this chaos that brought Napoleon into the limelight. In 1793 the port of Toulon rebelled against the government, and an army in which Napoleon was commander of artillery was sent to besiege the town. It was Napoleon's plan that led to its capture on 18 December. Two years later, on 5 November 1795 in Paris, he saved the Convention from an attack by royalists. Such episodes, and his marriage to Josephine de Beauharnais, who knew Director Barras well, led to his appointment in 1796 as commander-in-chief of the army to invade Italy.

His victories over the Austrians in Italy in 1796 and 1797 turned him into a national hero. He forced the Austrians to accept peace and in 1797 the treaty of Campo Formio was signed. France acquired the Austrian Netherlands, the left bank of the Rhine, and set up the Cisalpine Republic in northern Italy; Austria received Venice.

Since he was so popular, and because in 1797 he had saved the Directory from a possible royalist *coup*, the failure of the Egyptian campaign in 1798 and 1799 did not seriously damage Napoleon's prestige. By now he had developed political ambitions, and believed that he had the ability to govern France.

When he joined Sieyès and Ducos in the overthrow of the Directory in 1799, his chance had come.

The New Constitution: Napoleon in Power

Although in theory Sieyès, Ducos and Napoleon were jointly responsible for a new constitution, it was mainly Sieyès' ideas that were followed.

Most power was put into the hands of a First Consul, who would be advised by two other Consuls. They would be elected every ten years. The Consuls could propose laws, were in charge of the armed forces, finance, and appointed all state officers.

The legislative authority was made weak. Legislation was put into the hands of three assemblies; the Senate, the Tribunate, and the Legislative Assembly. None of these individually had much authority.

The French people voted to accept the Constitution in January 1800. Napoleon became First Consul. This in itself made him the most powerful man in France, but he was to strengthen his position when he became Consul for Life in 1802, and Emperor in 1804.

Admiral Nelson (1758–1805).

Napoleon and France

Napoleon's greatest reforms in France occurred while he was First Consul. Between 1800 and 1804 he introduced measures that left a deep mark on the country.

The Administrative System

Napoleon ruled France personally and his chief body of administration was the Council of State. Napoleon chose its members. At the local level only two administrative areas were retained: the Departments, run by Prefects appointed by Napoleon; the Communes, run by Mayors, many of whom were also appointed by Napoleon.

Church and State

Napoleon wished to heal the split between France and the papacy, and between those French clergy who had sworn loyalty to the state and those who had not. If he could do this his personal prestige would benefit, the whole Catholic Church would become a supporter of the government, and France would have more influence in Catholic Europe. The pope, Pius VII, desired good relations with France, and an end to the schism in the French Church.

After negotiations a Concordat was signed in 1801. The pope recognised the French Republic, abandoned all claims to Church property seized since 1789, agreed that the state would choose

The title page of the *Code Civil* or *Code Napoléon*.

CODE CIVIL

DES

FRANÇAIS.

ÉDITION ORIGINALE ET SEULE OFFICIELLE.

À PARIS,
DE L'IMPRIMERIE DE LA RÉPUBLIQUE.
AN XII. 1804.

The battle of Trafalgar.

chel Ney, duke of Elchingen,
nce of the Moskva
769–1815). He entered the
nch army as a private in 1787,
d rose through the ranks to
come a marshal in 1804; he
ght with great distinction at
h battles as Jena, Borodino
d Lutzen; in 1814 he submitted
Louis XVIII, and in 1815 he
s sent with an army to capture
poleon; he deserted with his
y to Napoleon and fought
ide him at Waterloo; he was
tured and shot for treason in
cember 1815.

bishops whom he could then invest, and allowed the clergy to
be paid by the state. Napoleon recognised Catholicism as 'the
religion of the great majority of citizens', although not as the
official state religion.

Napoleon did not stop there. Without consulting the pope he
added certain clauses (the Organic Articles) to the Concordat.
These stated that the bishops would be under the control of
the Prefects, and that no papal bull could be published or papal
agent operate in France without the government's consent.
Pius protested but could do nothing. The Catholic Church was
now effectively bound to the state, although united once more.

The Legal System

Before the Revolution the laws of France had been in great
disorder. In 1804 the task of producing a single legal code,
which had continued throughout the Revolution, was completed.
It is known as the 'Code Napoléon' and contained 2,281 articles.
Certain principles of the Revolution were upheld in the Code,
such as equality before the law and religious toleration; others
were altered, for judges were to be appointed by the government (not elected), and the use of the jury system was reduced.
The code not only became French law but was introduced in
other parts of Europe when Napoleon created the empire.

These measures, to which were added financial and educational reforms, turned France into a well-organised, centralised
state. Never had France been so prepared for efficient government by one man.

Napoleon and Europe: Peace and War 1801–7

When Napoleon came to power he inherited a war. In order
to concentrate on internal reforms he needed peace. Russia had

Jerome Bonaparte, king of Westphalia, 1807 and his wife Catherine.

Tsar Alexander I.

withdrawn from the war in 1799, and after defeats in 1800 Austria signed peace at Lunéville in 1801. Britain was war weary and signed peace with France in 1802 at Amiens.

War with Britain broke out again in 1803. Napoleon gathered an army at Boulogne, apparently to invade Britain although nobody knows whether he was serious. In any case an invasion was made impossible by two events: in August 1805 Austria and Russia joined Britain in the war against France, and Napoleon was forced to march against them; in October 1805 a British fleet under Nelson destroyed the French fleet at the battle of Trafalgar, and so gave Britain mastery of the seas.

A week before Trafalgar, Napoleon defeated the Austrians at Ulm and entered Vienna. In December he followed this up with the greatest of his victories over a joint Russian-Austrian army at Austerlitz. At the end of the month the Austrians signed peace at Pressburg.

In 1805 Prussia had refused to sign an alliance with Britain, Austria and Russia. Now she took fright and in 1806 declared war on France. This was an act of folly. In October 1806 Napoleon overcame the Prussians at the battle of Jena and marched into Berlin. The Prussian king, Frederick William III, had fled to Königsberg, and ordered his remaining troops to join the Russians. Napoleon therefore pushed eastwards, caught the Russians and Prussians at Eylau in February 1807

French soldiers burn British goods, 1810.

and once more defeated them. In June 1807 he completed the rout of his enemies when he beat the Russians at the battle of Friedland. Prussia and Russia had to make peace. The tsar, Alexander I, came personally to meet Napoleon at Tilsit, and in July 1807 terms were signed between France, Prussia and Russia. Napoleon now controlled almost the whole of Europe. What was he to do with it?

The Empire

Napoleon organised Europe into three parts. First there was the French Empire. Under Napoleon, France's frontiers expanded

Europe in 1810.

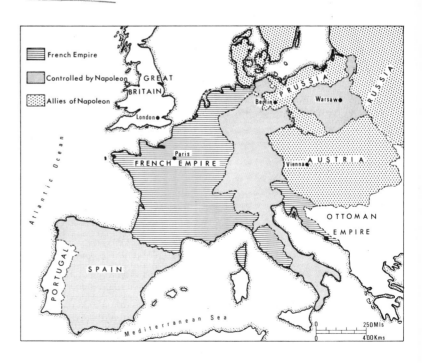

A painting by Goya showing Spaniards being executed by French soldiers in 1808.

Joachim Murat (1767–1815). Handsome and dashing, he was Napoleon's most brilliant cavalry commander; Napoleon rewarded him by allowing him to marry into the Bonaparte family, and by making him king of Naples in 1808; he deserted to the allies after Napoleon's defeats in 1813, but in 1815 threw in his lot with Napoleon again; he was captured and shot in October 1815 while trying to win back his kingdom.

and between 1805 and 1811 she annexed Piedmont, Tuscany, Illyria, the Papal States and Holland.

Then there was the Grand Empire: states not directly ruled from France but closely bound to it. These territories were often ruled by members of Napoleon's family. His stepson Eugene governed the kingdom of Italy; in 1806 his brother Louis was made king of Holland; in 1806 another brother, Joseph, became king of Naples and in 1808 king of Spain; in 1807 his younger brother Jerome was made king of Westphalia. Sometimes he stepped in himself, as when he became Protector of the Confederation of the Rhine, a group of sixteen Rhineland states formed in 1806. Again, he might use a supporter, such as the king of Saxony whom he made Grand Duke of Warsaw.

As for the rest of Europe, it was linked to France by a system of alliances. For example, in 1807 Russia and Denmark signed alliances with France, and in 1810 Austria and Sweden did so.

Napoleon's Imperial Policy

Napoleon hoped to make the Grand Empire popular with its subjects by introducing aspects of the French Revolution.

He abolished feudalism by 1811. The only exception was the Duchy of Warsaw, where serfdom was done away with, but the aristocrats kept some of their rights and privileges.

The Code Napoléon was applied throughout the Empire by 1812; this was partly for practical reasons, for Napoleon needed large numbers of civil servants to run the Grand Empire; the Code, which established equality of opportunity, allowed people of talent from all classes to acquire posts in administration.

uring the retreat from Russia, e French army, here seen ossing the river Beresina, ffered terrible losses.

e solemn re-entry of Louis XVIII o Paris, 3 May 1814.

e battle of Waterloo.

The states within the Grand Empire adopted constitutions based upon the French Constitution of 1799. Although there were some differences between them, they all kept the legislative authority weak, and followed the French system in financial, judicial and military affairs.

Throughout the Grand Empire the Church was subjected to the state. Once more there were some differences; in Westphalia the state seized church property, but in the Duchy of Warsaw it did not. Nevertheless, basically the French pattern was repeated.

The Continental System

Napoleon used the Grand Empire and his alliances to try to ruin the British economy and so force Britain to make peace. Between 1806 and 1810 he passed a series of edicts, the most important being the Berlin Decrees of 1806 and the Milan Decrees of 1807, which closed all the ports of Europe to British trade. He hoped that France would take over commerce lost to Britain through this Continental System, and become more prosperous than ever before.

The practical problems of enforcing this System were many, and in fact it was only applied strictly from 1807 to 1808 and from 1810 to 1812. British goods continued to enter Europe through an elaborate smuggling system, and Britain partly made up the loss of European trade by extending her trade with South America.

Although the Continental System failed to ruin the British economy, it did inflict damage. This was especially true when the U.S.A. joined the boycott in 1808 and from 1811 to 1812. Unemployment spread among the industries of Yorkshire and Lancashire, and in 1811 and 1812 it was so widespread that rioting broke out.

The Nationalist Challenge to the Empire

The Grand Empire was built on a contradiction. France ruled Europe, but the French Revolution stated that sovereignty belonged to the people; this implied that Italy, for instance, should be ruled by the Italians themselves. As Napoleon imposed Revolutionary practices on Europe, the idea of the sovereignty of the people spread, and inevitably there were attempts to expel the French. This is how modern European nationalism began. Nationalist risings occurred in Italy in 1806, and anti-French secret societies were formed in Germany.

The nationalist challenge was particularly strong in Spain. In 1808 Napoleon made his brother Joseph king of Spain, a decision that provoked a strong nationalist uprising. In 1807 the French had invaded Portugal, but Britain sent troops under

Louis Bonaparte, king of Holland, 1806.

Joseph Bonaparte, king of Naples, 1806 and king of Spain, 1808.

The last portion of Napoleon's will signed by him in 1821.

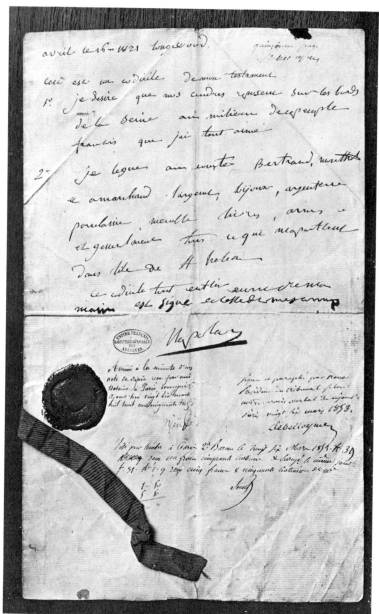

Arthur Wellesley, duke of Wellington (1769–1852). Born in Ireland he received part of his military training in France; in 1809 he was put in command of the British army in the Peninsular war, where his successes earned him his dukedom; he acted as a British representative at the Congress of Vienna and was made commander-in-chief of the allied armies at Waterloo; later he concentrated on politics and was prime minister of Britain from 1828–30.

Wellesley (who later became the duke of Wellington) to aid the Portuguese. The French were thus fighting two wars in this part of Europe, and the Peninsular war, as the two struggles are called, lasted until 1814, and forced Napoleon to keep 300,000 troops in Spain.

Anti-French feeling was even more inflamed by the Continental System. People objected to European commerce being reorganised for the benefit of France.

Negotiators at the Congress of Vienna. Wellington is on the extreme left, Metternich is standing in front of the chair (centre left), Castlereagh is seated with left arm over the back of the chair (centre Talleyrand is seated with right arm on the table (right).

The Russian Campaign

Meanwhile relations with Russia declined, mainly because Russia refused to support the Continental System. Since Russia was not under direct French control, the only way to force her to obey French policy was by war. Napoleon collected an army of 400,000 men and in June 1812 set out to invade Russia. He pushed into Russia and in September 1812 seized Moscow. It was an empty city for the inhabitants had fled. The Russian government refused to make peace, so that Napoleon had military but not political victory. He stayed in Moscow for five weeks, but then had to retreat as winter was approaching. Also Moscow had burnt to the ground, for fires had broken out; since the city was built mainly of wood, and the usual fire-fighting services had fled, there was no way of saving it. Disease, starvation, and attacks by the Russians took a terrible toll of the French army, and although it managed to reach the Duchy of Warsaw before the full grip of winter was felt, only 100,000 men returned.

The Collapse of the Empire

Napoleon's old enemies took the chance to strike. In 1813 Russia, Austria and Prussia allied with Britain. His best soldiers gone, Napoleon gathered another army and met the allies at the battle of Leipzig in October 1813. He was defeated. The allies headed for France; by the end of the year Wellington had overrun Spain and crossed the Pyrenees; in January 1814 the Austrians, Russians and Prussians invaded France. On 31 March Paris surrendered and on 6 April Napoleon abdicated and was exiled to Elba. The French monarchy was restored and Louis XVI's brother became Louis XVIII.

The carousel—one of the indoor entertainments during the congress.

Napoleon was not yet finished. He escaped from Elba and on 1 March 1815 arrived back in France. He mustered an army, recovered Paris, and on 18 June met an allied army under the duke of Wellington at the battle of Waterloo. Once more he was defeated and sent into exile; this time to the island of St. Helena in the Atlantic, where he died in 1821.

The Congress of Vienna

The overthrow of Napoleon's empire meant that Europe had to be reconstructed. This was done at the Congress of Vienna from November 1814 to June 1815. All the European states sent representatives but the major powers, Austria, Britain, Russia and Prussia, dominated the Congress.

Entertainment was organised for visitors to the congress. This sleigh ride took place on 22 January 1815.

Peace with France had been settled in May 1814. The terms agreed that France should return to the frontiers of 1 January 1792, and should keep most of her colonies. After Waterloo these terms were altered; France lost Savoy, had to pay war damages, and was to be occupied by 150,000 allied troops for at least three years.

Other parts of Europe were put under the control of one or more of the great powers. Most of Germany was turned into a Confederation of thirty-nine states; Austria and Prussia were members, although not all of their territory lay within its frontiers. Italy was divided into eight states; four were taken by Austria, three were given to the pope (but Austria could keep troops in them), and the state of Piedmont-Sardinia, which included Nice and Savoy, was restored. Poland was recreated, but put under the control of Russia.

These were the major territorial arrangements. Further agreements were the creation of a united kingdom of Holland (including modern Holland and Belgium), the unification of Norway and Sweden, and Britain's acquisition of such territories as Malta, the Cape of Good Hope, Ceylon and islands in the West Indies.

Europe in 1815.

Death mask of Napoleon.

Things to Do

1. Write a character study of Napoleon.
2. Find out what aspects of Napoleon's reforms carried on into nineteenth and twentieth century France.
3. Find out more about the Peninsular war. What effect did it have on France?
4. What were the strong and weak points of the Congress of Vienna?

Books to Read or Consult

N. Hampson, *The First European Revolution, 1776-1815,* London 1969.

F. M. H. Markham, *Napoleon and the Awakening of Europe,* London 1954.

F. M. H. Markham, *Napoleon,* London 1963.

A. Palmer, *Napoleon in Russia,* London 1967.

J. M. Thompson, *Napoleon Bonaparte, his Rise and Fall,* Oxford 1952.

Gebhard Lebrecht von Blücher (1742–1819). A German who served in both the Swedish and Prussian armies; in 1815 he commanded the Prussian army to fight Napoleon; although defeated by Napoleon at Ligny on 16 June he arrived on the battlefield at Waterloo on the evening of 18 June and decided the battle in favour of Wellington.

The Industrial Revolution in Europe

European life was not only profoundly changed by the political upheaval of the French Revolution and its consequences, but also by the Industrial Revolution. The phrase 'Industrial Revolution' must be treated with care. Industrialisation did not occur overnight. It began in the second half of the eighteenth century, but nowhere reached large-scale proportions until at least the 1840s. New inventions were often adopted slowly, so that traditional means of production lasted well into the nineteenth century. Furthermore, industrialisation did not equally affect the whole of Europe. Although industry in Britain was well developed by the 1840s, parts of eastern Europe, and Russia in particular, did not become widely industrialised until the middle of the present century.

The Causes of Industrialisation

The Industrial Revolution was the result of a number of developments which unfolded at the same time.

Growth of Population

The population of Europe continued to grow throughout the nineteenth century. In 1800 there were about 190 million Europeans, and by 1870 this figure had risen to 310 millions. Certain countries can be taken to illustrate this:

James Watt.

Country	Years	Rise in Population (in millions)
Britain	1811–70	19—31.5
France	1815–60	29—38
Netherlands	1829–67	2.6—3.5

There was also a general movement from the countryside into the towns. In 1800 there were only twenty-two towns in Europe with a population over 100,000, but in 1850 there were forty-seven. By 1870, 50% of the German population lived in towns, 33% of the French, and 65% of the British. The reasons for this movement are complex and owed a great deal to local conditions; the growth of some English towns in the 1840s, for example, was helped by the influx of outsiders, many of whom were Irishmen. There were general reasons, however, such as the tendency for wages in towns to be higher

Watt's rotative beam engine.

than in the countryside, and the fact that agricultural crises forced people to leave rural areas.

The enlarged population meant a steady supply of workers to industry and more customers for manufactured goods.

Mechanisation

From the 1750s onwards machines were invented that allowed existing industries to expand and encouraged the foundation of new ones. The first important machine of the Industrial Revolution was the steam engine. Developed by Thomas Newcomen in 1705, it was employed at first solely for pumping water, but was more widely used by 1712. In 1781 James Watt produced a much improved version which could drive machinery directly. The steam engine was used mainly, although not entirely, in the textiles industry in the eighteenth century, but its use spread in the nineteenth. The steam engine is but one aspect of mechanisation; later in the chapter reference will be made to other types of machinery.

Growth of Overseas Trade

During the eighteenth and nineteenth centuries European countries, Britain most of all, expanded their trade with the rest of the world. Thus an even larger market for manufactured goods was created, a factor which encouraged the Industrial Revolution. The rate at which overseas trade grew is shown in the rise in exports from different countries.

Country	Years	Growth of Exports
Britain	1820–70	1,000%
France	1827–69	560%
Belgium	1836–66	480%

The growth of exports led to the expansion of shipbuilding as more and more ships were needed to carry goods overseas. Britain once more led the way. In 1815 the total tonnage of British merchant ships was almost 2,500,000 tons; by 1875 it had risen to nearly 6,300,000 tons, or 40% of the world total. France is another example. In 1837 the tonnage of her merchant ships came to 685,000 tons, and in 1867 reached 1,000,000 tons.

There were improvements in the type of ship that was built, the chief development being the steamship. The earliest steamships were built in the 1780s, but were well established by 1818 when William Denny introduced the *Rob Roy* on a regular service between Glasgow and Belfast. Until the 1830s steamships were driven by paddle; there might be one at the stern, or one on each side of the vessel. In the 1830s screw propellers were developed, and for a time used together with the paddle. By the end of the 1860s, however, the screw propeller was used alone since it was more efficient than the paddle.

International trade was also aided by the construction of interocean canals which greatly reduced the distances that ships had to travel. The Suez Canal, built by the French engineer Ferdinand de Lesseps, was opened in 1869; it reduced the sea journey between India and Europe by 4,000 miles. In Europe itself there was built between 1887 and 1895 the Kiel Canal, which crossed southern Denmark and linked the North Sea with the Baltic. On the American continent the Panama Canal was built. It was started by de Lesseps, but because of many difficulties it was not completed until 1914; it shortened the routes between the west coast of America and Europe by almost 6,000 miles.

The *Comet,* an early steamship built in 1811.

An early passenger steamboat.

The *Great Eastern* steamship was 695 ft. long and used both screw propeller and paddles.

62

Developments in Basic Materials

The principal materials of the Industrial Revolution were coal and iron. Coal increasingly was used as a source of power, until by the middle of the nineteenth century it was the main source of energy for Europe's industry. In the most industrially advanced parts of Europe, coal production figures for 1836 are as follows:

Country	Coal (tons)
Britain	25,000,000
France	2,500,000
Belgium	7,000,000

These figures are a good guide to the extent to which these three countries were industrialised.

Iron was essential to many products of the industrial age. Machines, railways, bridges, and factories are only a few examples of the use of iron. In Britain, France and Belgium smelted iron was produced at these rates:

	Years	Smelted Iron Ore (tons)
Britain	1806–40	258,000—1,400,000
Britain	1840–70	1,400,000—6,700,000
France	1824–70	198,000—1,178,000
Belgium	1836	50,000

The Spread of Railways

Many historians say that the combined effect of the developments just outlined did not in themselves make the Industrial Revolution, but simply amounted to industrial change. The turning point came with the spread of railways; they turned

The opening of the Suez Canal in 1869.

64

Richard Trevithick invented the first steam-powered vehicle for carrying passengers. He demonstrated it at Euston Square in London in 1808.

Arthur Young (1741–1820). An enthusiastic supporter of the New Agriculture, he began a series of tours in 1767 in which he studied farming in England, Ireland and France as well as other places; he was in Paris during the Revolution (see p. 27); he published accounts of his travels in such works as his *Tour in Ireland* (1780) and his *Travels in France* (1792).

industrial change into the Industrial Revolution. They gave Europe better communications than ever before, and allowed raw materials and manufactured goods to be transported quickly, and in large quantities, throughout the continent.

The construction of railways on an extensive scale came in the 1830s and 1840s. During that period many of the principal networks that still exist were laid. In 1830 there were only a few miles of railway in Europe, mostly in Britain; by 1854 there were 14,000 miles, and by 1871, 59,500 miles.

The European Industrial Revolution was marked by these general features. It has been said that Britain enjoyed the lead, and she held it for most of the nineteenth century. The situation in Britain can be examined in order to understand why she was able to set the pace.

British Agriculture

British agriculture created conditions within which industrialisation could flourish by keeping the supply of food at a high level. Since there was no shortage, food prices remained reasonable, and Britain avoided much of the widespread social discontent that existed in France. The production of food remained adequate, partly because there were good harvests between 1720 and the 1760s, but also because agricultural techniques slowly improved, and more land was cultivated.

New Techniques

One of the great pioneers in the improvement of agricultural methods was Jethro Tull, who studied crops. He replaced the

The seed drill invented by Jethro Tull. The boxes were filled with seeds and as the wheels went around they worked a mechanism which allowed the seeds to drop out at a steady rate.

traditional method of sowing broadcast by one in which seeds were carefully sown in rows. For this purpose he invented in 1701 a seed drill which bored a small hole in the ground and dropped a seed into it. He also found that the ground in which seeds were planted needed to be hoed regularly, and in 1714 he invented the horse hoe for this purpose.

Viscount Charles Townshend is another notable figure. After he retired to his Norfolk estates in 1730 he popularised agricultural techniques already being used in that county. He increased the quantity of his crops by avoiding the traditional fallow year. Instead, he followed four-crop rotation as was the practice in Norfolk. He found that with a four years programme of wheat, turnips, barley and clover, land could be used continually. Four-crop rotation also meant that animal foods as well as human foods could be grown in large quantities. Townshend was also concerned with land improvement. Broad areas of his estates consisted mainly of sand, which he was able to turn into productive soil by working in marl (a clay and lime mixture); this became a standard way to reclaim sandy soil.

Improvements in animal breeding took place, much work being done by Robert Bakewell between 1760 and 1790. He selected his breeding animals carefully, and developed the New Leicestershire sheep which gave more wool and meat than previous breeds, and bigger cattle such as the New Leicestershire Shorthorn. A measure of the success of his ideas is the fact that between 1710 and 1795 at the Southfield livestock fair near to his home, the average weight of sheep rose from 28 pounds to 80 pounds, and the average weight of cattle from 370 pounds to 800 pounds.

It should not be imagined that improvements like this made an immediate impact on agriculture. Change was a slow process, for many farmers were happy to continue old-fashioned methods. Attempts were made to propagate the 'New Agri-

1710: 370 lb.

1795: 800 lb.

1710: 28 lb.

1795: 80 lb.

66

A mechanical reaper being used on an experimental farm in France about the middle of the nineteenth century.

culture', as it was called, and nobody made more strenuous efforts than Arthur Young. In his published accounts of his tours through England, Ireland, France and Italy, he paid careful attention to the agricultural practices that he had observed. In 1784 he began to publish the *Annals of Agriculture,* a journal that upheld new techniques, and in 1793 he was appointed secretary to the Board of Agriculture, a post that he used to spread new ideas.

Enclosures

The tendency for more land to be brought under cultivation was bound up with the enclosure movement. Enclosures were already well under way at the beginning of the eighteenth century, for by 1700 about half of the arable land in England had been enclosed.

One way for enclosure to take place was for a wealthy land-owner simply to purchase the land of smaller farmers that was mixed up with his own. He then enclosed the whole area with hedges and fences and worked the land as he wished.

The New Leicestershire sheep.

Another way was for the landowner to apply to Parliament for permission to enclose land. Commissioners were then appointed to investigate the claim. If it were accepted, the commissioners allotted compact areas to each landowner in the region concerned, in place of scattered strips in open fields. Applications usually were accepted for many Members of Parliament were themselves landowners, supporters of the New Agriculture, and sympathisers with the enclosure movement. Between 1700 and 1845 about 4,000 enclosure acts were passed and they enclosed about 6 million acres. By the mid-1840s almost all of the arable land in England had been enclosed.

It used to be thought that enclosures had a disastrous effect on the rural population. It was said that enclosures forced farmers out of business, took away villagers' pasture rights and put large numbers of farm labourers out of work. Historians now take a somewhat different view. It is true that many country people were moving into the towns, but there is no proof that it was those parts of the country where enclosures were common that lost their population. It has also been shown that the larger, enclosed farms needed more and more men to work on them, and often offered increased employment to farm labourers. It can no longer be said that enclosures were an automatic calamity for the rural population.

Surveyors measuring land for enclosure at Henlow in the count of Bedford, about 1798.

Richard Arkwright.

The Expansion of British Industry

Agriculture created suitable conditions for industrialisation, but other factors contributed too. Labour was mobile, that is to say that where industry grew, people could go and work. This was not the case everywhere in the eighteenth century. In Russia, for instance, the serf was bound to the land and could not leave his village unless his lord agreed. In Britain there was no such problem. People could work where they wished.

A picture of 'mule' spinning which shows how much the amount of cloth produced must have been increased by this new method.

Again, although Britain was involved in wars in the eighteenth century, almost no fighting took place in Britain itself. The only exceptions are the Jacobite risings of 1715 and 1745. Consequently the country was not ravaged by war as other parts of Europe were. Indeed, war turned out to be a profitable business, for Britain emerged from the wars with an enlarged empire. Even the Napoleonic wars helped industry. In spite of the Continental System, Britain developed her world trade, her industries were stimulated by the demand for war goods, and the wars removed her European commercial rivals.

Against this background, British industry began to spread rapidly in the 1770s. Expansion was most marked in cotton and iron.

A power loom operator at work.

The Cotton Industry

The cotton industry was already well established in the eighteenth century, but it was now stimulated by a growing demand for cotton goods, and by a number of technical improvements that enabled it to increase output.

A step towards mechanisation had been taken in 1733 when John Kay invented the fly shuttle. This enabled a weaver to double his production, but made little impression and was not widely used until the 1750s and 1760s.

From the 1760s technical changes occurred in spinning. In 1764 James Hargreaves built the spinning jenny, which enabled a spinner to work eight spindles instead of one. Bigger models were made, and by 1800 jennies could hold up to 100 spindles. Another aid was the spinning (or water) frame constructed by Richard Arkwright in 1769. Driven by water, it twisted the cotton as it came through the frame, and so produced a strong thread which allowed manufacturers to make cloth entirely of cotton; formerly cotton thread had been weak and had to be mixed with linen. Spinning also profited from Samuel Crompton's 'mule' of 1779, which combined the jenny and the frame, and not only spun large amounts of cotton, but also made an extremely fine, high quality cloth. In 1785 steam power was first applied to these machines, and thereafter manufacturers increasingly drove them by steam.

As for the weaving side of the cotton industry, Edmund Cartwright invented a power loom in 1784. It eventually replaced the hand loom, but the change took place slowly.

In 1760 the cotton industry had been a minor one, but the growth of demand and production turned it into the largest in Britain by 1810.

The loom-shed at Halifax shows how the power loom was used for factory production.

A spinning wheel operator at work before the new mechanical inventions.

A reproduction of James Hargreaves' spinning jenny. The operator worked it by turning the handle at the side.

71

Arkwright's improved spinning machine, about 1775.

The Cloth Hall at Leeds, one of the centres for the sale of cloth.

Section of a charcoal blast furnace. Iron ore contains other substances as well as iron. To extract the iron, great heat is applied to the ore which melts. The other materials, known as 'slag', float to the top and are poured off leaving the iron. This process is called 'smelting'.

The Iron Industry

The growth of the iron industry in Britain followed a similar path to that of cotton; the demand grew, and technical improvements allowed the industry to meet the demand.

Until the first decade of the eighteenth century the smelting process was fired by charcoal. In 1709 Abraham Darby had used coke instead of charcoal, but the practice did not become widespread until the 1770s. Coke did not burn easily and therefore it was difficult to get it to the necessary temperature for smelting to take place. Even as late as 1776 there were only thirty-one coke furnaces in Britain.

A solution came in 1761 with the invention of the air pump which gave a strong blast of air capable of allowing coke to burn at a high temperature. When this proved successful coke became more widely used, much to the relief of the iron masters,

The molten iron is drawn off from the blast furnace through channels called 'pigs' and is known as pig iron. It still contains impurities which make it very brittle. These are burned off in the process known as 'puddling'.

73

for supplies of wood were running down and therefore the cost of using charcoal as fuel was rising.

The shortage of charcoal created a further problem. Pig iron had to be reheated for further refining under the blows of a hammer worked by a water wheel. The forges where this was done had difficulty in acquiring enough charcoal. The problem was overcome by several people, the most famous being Henry Cort, who in 1784 devised the puddling and rolling process. Molten metal in the furnace was raked (puddled) to remove unwanted substances, and then put through rollers driven by steam power. This double treatment produced high quality iron.

These measures enabled the iron industry to step up its output. Between 1788 and 1806 production rose fourfold.

Puddled iron is hammered and rolled in a forge to remove remaining liquid slag. In this more workable form it is called 'wrought' or 'bar' iron.

Communications

Up to the 1820s only the cotton and iron industries had shown signs of dramatic expansion or revolution. As elsewhere in Europe it was the coming of the railways that enabled industry as a whole to be revolutionised. Before the railways arrived, however, communications had already been improving in the eighteenth century.

Canals

A considerable amount of canal building had taken place. One of the great engineers was James Brindley who did much

The Irwell aqueduct. This was a bridge by which the canal, built by James Brindley for the duke of Bridgewater, was carried across the river Irwell.

In 1856 Henry Bessemer invented a way of producing steel cheaply. The molten pig iron was poured directly into a converter (the large containers on left and right) and a blast of hot air was blown through holes in the bottom. The impurities were burned off as gas or became liquid slag. Small amounts of carbon and manganese were added to make 'mild' steel.

work for the duke of Bridgewater. The duke owned coal mines at Worsley, near Manchester, and in 1761 Brindley built a canal seven miles long between the mine and Manchester. Another noteworthy Brindley canal was the Grand Trunk Canal that linked the Midlands with northern England.

Canal building went ahead on an ambitious scale, and between 1758 and 1807 Parliament passed 165 acts authorising their construction. By 1830 England south of York had a network of navigable waterways totalling 4,000 miles.

Canals had advantages over other modes of transport since they enabled goods to be moved in bulk, they reduced transport costs by as much as 80%, and they made manufactured goods and raw materials available over a wider area than ever before.

The west county mails set out from Piccadilly in London, about 1830.

Roads

Roads too were improved, and two kinds of problem had to be overcome. First was the question of raising labour and money. Eighteenth century England simply kept the seventeenth century turnpike trust going. The trusts were groups of local citizens, people such as farmers, traders, landlords and clergy, who took charge of certain stretches of road. They had the right to borrow money for building roads, hiring labour, and collecting tolls to offset the costs. By 1830 there were 1,100 turnpike trusts in England, and they were responsible for over 20,000 miles of road. Most of them disbanded in the 1830s since they were badly organised and short of money.

The duke of Bridgewater

The other problem was practical; the quality of roads badly needed to be improved. Various experiments were tried, but the type of road that became the most commonly accepted, and which is standard to this day, was developed in Italy and intro-duced to Britain by Thomas Telford and John McAdam. The procedure was to lay a strong foundation by dumping large stones on the bed of the road, the large stones were then covered with smaller stones, and they in turn were topped with gravel or slag. In order to help drainage, the centre of the road was made higher than the sides, and ditches were dug alongside.

Travel by heavy coach in the eighteenth century was slow and uncomfortable. Five or six people travel inside this coach. One of those travelling on the roof is a sailor, while an old woman, smoking a pipe, rides with the luggage in the basket. The coach went about twenty-eight miles per day and it cost 2d. per mile to travel inside, 1d. per mile outside.

The old horses in this Cruikshank drawing of 1829 watch the 'coach without horses' or steam carriage. This invention was prevented from developing by high road tolls.

The mail coach loses a wheel causing the passengers some discomfort.

A model of Richard Trevithick's steam locomotive, 1804.

This kind of road was immensely successful. It was harder wearing than other roads and greatly eased travel. The average speed of coaches rose from four miles per hour to nine or ten miles per hour on the smooth surface. Heavier loads could be pulled since the surface allowed wagons and carts to run easily. Travel by night became possible, for coaches were not now liable to tumble into a hole or pool of mud. The coach journey from Edinburgh to London, which took fourteen days on the old roads, took only forty-four hours on the new ones.

Railways

Railways had been used in industry as early as the seventeenth century, when trucks set on rails of wood were pulled by horses. In the late 1700s and early 1800s tests were carried out on the employment of steam as a source of motion. A successful steam locomotive was built as early as 1804 by Richard Trevithick. It was George Stephenson who applied the steam locomotive to public transport. In 1825 his engine *Rocket* (it was capable of thirty miles per hour) pulled passengers between Stockton and Darlington, and a regular service started. A more profitable passenger service was set up between Manchester and Liverpool in 1830.

In the 1830s a fever of railway building occurred, especially in 1836 and 1837 when 1,000 miles of rail were laid, and large amounts of money were invested. The railway builders faced a multitude of problems. Money had to be raised, parliamentary permission had to be acquired before lines could be constructed, there were immense technical problems to be overcome, and there was opposition from canal and stagecoach companies who rightly feared that the railways would destroy their business.

In 1829 the Grand Competition of Locomotives on the Liverpool and Manchester Railway took place. The directors of the railway offered a prize of £500 for the most improved locomotive engine. Stephenson's *Rocket* won having reached a speed of twenty-nine miles per hour.

78

1829.

GRAND COMPETITION
of
LOCOMOTIVES
on the
LIVERPOOL & MANCHESTER RAILWAY.

STIPULATIONS & CONDITIONS

On which the Directors of the Liverpool and Manchester Railway offer a Premium of £500 for the most improved Locomotive Engine.

I.

The said Engine must "effectually consume its own smoke," according to the provisions of the Railway Act, 7th Geo. IV.

II.

The Engine, if it weighs Six Tons, must be capable of drawing after it, day by day, on a well-constructed Railway, on a level plane, a Train of Carriages of the gross weight of Twenty Tons, including the Tender and Water Tank, at the rate of Ten Miles per Hour, with a pressure of steam in the boiler not exceeding Fifty Pounds on the square inch.

III.

There must be Two Safety Valves, one of which must be completely out of the reach or control of the Engine-man, and neither of which must be fastened down while the Engine is working.

IV.

The Engine and Boiler must be supported on Springs, and rest on Six Wheels; and the height from the ground to the top of the Chimney must not exceed Fifteen Feet.

V.

The weight of the Machine, WITH ITS COMPLEMENT OF WATER in the Boiler, must, at most, not exceed Six Tons, and a Machine of less weight will be preferred if it draw AFTER it a PROPORTIONATE weight; and if the weight of the Engine, &c., do not exceed FIVE TONS, then the gross weight to be drawn need not exceed Fifteen Tons: and in that proportion for Machines of still smaller weight—provided that the Engine, &c., shall still be on six wheels, unless the weight (as above) be reduced to Four Tons and a Half, or under, in which case the Boiler, &c., may be placed on four wheels. And the Company shall be at liberty to put the Boiler, Fire Tube, Cylinders, &c., to the test of a pressure of water not exceeding 150 Pounds per square inch, without being answerable for any damage the Machine may receive in consequence.

VI.

There must be a Mercurial Gauge affixed to the Machine, with Index Rod, showing the Steam Pressure above 45 Pounds per square inch; and constructed to blow out a Pressure of 60 Pounds per inch.

VII.

The Engine to be delivered complete for trial, at the Liverpool end of the Railway, not later than the 1st of October next.

VIII.

The price of the Engine which may be accepted, not to exceed £550, delivered on the Railway; and any Engine not approved to be taken back by the Owner.

N.B.—The Railway Company will provide the Engine Tender with a supply of Water and Fuel, for the experiment. The distance within the Rails is four feet eight inches and a half.

THE LOCOMOTIVE STEAM ENGINES,
WHICH COMPETED FOR THE PRIZE OF £500 OFFERED BY THE DIRECTORS OF THE LIVERPOOL AND MANCHESTER RAILWAY COMPANY.
DRAWN TO A SCALE ¼ INCH TO A FOOT.

THE "ROCKET" OF Mr. ROBt STEPHENSON OF NEWCASTLE.
WHICH DRAWING A LOAD EQUIVALENT TO THREE TIMES ITS WEIGHT TRAVELLED AT THE RATE OF 12½ MILES AN HOUR, AND WITH A CARRIAGE & PASSENGERS AT THE RATE OF 24 MILES. COST PER MILE FOR FUEL ABOUT THREE HALFPENCE.

THE "NOVELTY" OF MESSrs. BRAITHWAITE & ERRICSSON OF LONDON.
WHICH DRAWING A LOAD EQUIVALENT TO THREE TIMES ITS WEIGHT TRAVELLED AT THE RATE OF 20¾ MILES AN HOUR, AND WITH A CARRIAGE & PASSENGERS AT THE RATE OF 32 MILES. COST PER MILE FOR FUEL ABOUT ONE HALFPENNY.

THE "SANSPAREIL" OF Mr. HACKWORTH OF DARLINGTON.
WHICH DRAWING A LOAD EQUIVALENT TO THREE TIMES ITS WEIGHT TRAVELLED AT THE RATE OF 12½ MILES AN HOUR. COST FOR FUEL PER MILE ABOUT TWO PENCE.

Casting the nave of a railway carriage wheel.

Even so, the railways spread quickly and by 1848 there were 5,000 miles of rail in Britain.

The Industrial Revolution in Britain now went ahead at full pace, and Britain's trade with the rest of the world similarly grew. During most of the nineteenth century she led the world industrially and created immense wealth. By the end of the century, however, her industrial output was exceeded by Germany and the U.S.A. Although Britain remained a major industrial state in the twentieth century, she no longer enjoyed her supremacy of the 1800s.

In this chapter the Industrial Revolution has been considered only from the point of view of industry itself. It was just as important in the way in which it introduced severe social problems into European life. To this issue we now turn.

George Stephenson (1781–1848). As a boy he worked in a Northumberland colliery and studied at night school; he became interested in engineering and in 1814 built a locomotive that could draw eight loaded carriages at four miles per hour; after the opening of the Stockton to Darlington railway, he became the chief engineer on the Liverpool and Manchester railway that opened in 1830.

Things to Do
1. Take one aspect of the Industrial Revolution and find out what technical improvements were made. Trace their development to the twentieth century.
2. Read about the construction of the Suez and Panama canals.
3. Compare the extent to which the Industrial Revolution affected Ireland with one or more other countries.

The opening of the Stockton and Darlington Railway, 27 September 1825.

Books to Read or Consult

T. S. Ashton, *The Industrial Revolution, 1760-1830,* Oxford 1969.

H. Ellis, *British Railway History,* 2 vols., London 1954–9.

W. O. Henderson, *Britain and Industrial Europe,* Liverpool 1954.

W. O. Henderson, *The Industrial Revolution on the Continent,* London 1961.

G. Hogg, *Suez canal,* London 1969.

Social Problems of the Industrial Revolution

The greatest social problem raised by the Industrial Revolution concerns its impact on the industrial workers.

The Size of the Working Class

Care should be taken not to exaggerate the size of the working class, for even as late as the 1840s most industries operated on a small scale. Belgium was well developed industrially, but the average coal mine there employed only about 150 people, while a cotton mill employed about forty. It was after 1850 that the working class reached a sizeable proportion of the population in certain countries. The industrial workers were, of course, concentrated in industrial towns. Most of these were medium sized like Lille, Mulhouse and Rouen; industry in Europe (with the exception of Britain) rarely developed extensively in existing large cities.

Workers and Employers

Before the Industrial Revolution, industry was based on the cottage. Small groups of three or four people worked together and enjoyed close personal relations; there was little distinction between employer and employee. The Industrial Revolution changed this. As factories grew and more and more people were employed in them, the personal contact between employer and worker disappeared. Indeed a gulf opened between them, and many employers felt little concern for the welfare of their workers.

The Effect of Mechanisation

In the early stages of the Industrial Revolution mechanisation was seen as a threat to the workers. A single machine could do the task of several men, and employers dismissed workers as they used more machinery. In the 1820s and 1830s, and even later, mechanisation meant unemployment.

Even to those who kept their jobs, machines presented problems. In order to be as productive as possible machines often were run for twenty-four hours a day. Somebody had to be there to operate them, and workers therefore had to put in long hours, day and night. This applied to child workers as well as adults. In October 1830 Richard Oastler wrote a letter to the *Leeds Mercury* complaining that,

Alfred Krupp (1812–87). After inheriting his father's small workshop and the secret of how to make high quality steel, he built up the firm mainly by benefiting from the spread of railways; he introduced the Bessemer and open hearth processes to Europe, and cared for his workers by introducing welfare services for their benefit; his firm supplied artillery to the Prussian army and helped it to win the war against France from 1870–1.

82

Sheffield in 1858.

An early factory.

83

Children at work in a cotton mill about 1820.

Thousands of our fellow-creatures and fellow-subjects, both male and female, . . . are this very moment existing in a state of slavery, more horrid than are the victims of that hellish system 'colonial slavery'. . . . . Thousands of little children, both male and female, but principally female, from seven to fourteen years of age, are daily compelled to labour from six o'clock in the morning to seven in the evening, with only—Britons, blush while you read it!—with only thirty minutes allowed for eating and recreation.

In northern Italy a great deal of child labour was used. Many of these children were orphans or foundlings acquired by the factories from local hospitals. In Lombardy in 1840, 37,800 children were employed in industry, most of them working from twelve to fourteen hours a day. In 1843 regulations were introduced to control child labour there: children under nine were no longer to be employed, those under twelve were to work a maximum of ten hours a day and were to do no night work, children under fourteen were to do no more than twelve hours although this could be at night.

Children worked long hours even underground in the mines.

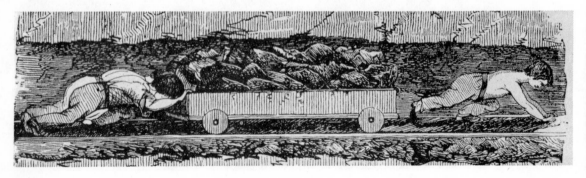

ners worked in cramped and
gerous conditions.

he 1820s and 1830s
chanisation meant
mployment.

men too worked in the mines.

Conditions of Work

The factories and mines were usually grim places. They were cramped, there was little ventilation, and the effect upon health was serious. In 1833 observers described conditions in British coal mines thus:

Labour very hard, nine hours a day regularly, sometimes twelve, sometimes above thirteen hours; stop two or three minutes to eat; some days nothing at all to eat; sometimes work and eat together; have worked a whole day together without stopping to eat; a good many children in the mines, some under six years of age; sometimes can't eat owing to the dust, and damp, and badness of the air; sometimes it is as hot as an oven, sometimes so hot as to melt a candle. A vast many girls in the pits go down just the same as the boys, by ladders or baskets; the girls wear breeches; beaten the same as the boys; . . . a good deal of fighting amongst them; much crookedness caused by the labour; work by candlelight; exposed to terrible accidents; work in very contracted spaces; children are plagued with sore feet and gatherings.

Wages

If the nineteenth century is taken as a whole, wages in industry rose higher than the rise in prices, and so the working class gradually grew richer. This was not a constant process, however, and there were several periods when workers' wages were low and even in decline; this happened in France in the 1820s. Even as late as 1848 in France, the average annual wages of the male industrial worker were only between 500 and 600 francs; to indicate how little this was worth, the average family spent about 120 francs a year on bread alone. In Wales in 1856, labourers earned about 12/– a week and miners about 14/– a week.

Living Conditions of the Working Class

The dwellings in which industrial workers lived were usually appalling. Sometimes old houses were taken over and people crowded in, one family per room. New workers' houses also were built. These were small, back-to-back terrace houses which lacked adequate windows, often had no running water, had no provision for the disposal of rubbish (which was simply dumped into the street), and had no flush-lavatories. These were built separately but in small numbers, a good example being one part of Manchester in the 1840s where there was one

Workers' houses were built nea the factory.

lavatory per 200 people. Many people lived in cellars. In Liverpool in 1839 almost 40,000 people lived in cellars at an average of five per cellar, and in London and New York also, thousands lived in basements.

The new houses were normally built near to the factory, and their tenants therefore suffered from the harmful waste products that the factory disgorged. Factory chimneys puffed out smoke and put ammonia, chlorine, carbon monoxide, and a host of other dangerous substances into the atmosphere. The factory dumped chemical wastes into nearby rivers, destroyed the life in them and made the water unfit for drinking or bathing. In 1862 Hugh Miller described the river Irwell at Manchester in this way:

The dwellings in which industri workers lived were usually appalling.

86

There are myriads of dirty things given it to wash, and whole wagon-loads of poisons from dye houses and bleachyards thrown into it to carry away; steam boilers discharge into it their seething contents, and drains and sewers their fetid impurities; till at length it rolls on—here between tall dingy walls, there under precipices of red sand-stone—considerably less a river than a flood of liquid manure.

Given such conditions, hygiene was impossible. The slums were infested with mice, rats, flies and lice. Cellars were damp and full of foul stenches. The streets were filled with rubbish, and the workers' pigs and chickens rooted among it.

Inevitably disease was rife. Children suffered from rickets, skin ailments, smallpox, scarlet fever, typhoid and other afflictions. There was a shocking infant mortality rate. In New York in 1810 it stood between 120 and 145 per 1,000 live births, and by 1870 the figure had risen to 240 per 1,000 live births. It has

87

London slums at the end of the
nineteenth century.

been calculated that in Liverpool in 1840 there were 6,000
deaths among the working class; the average age of these
people was only fifteen years, and almost 3,600 of them were
under five.

To many, the working class appeared little more than a slave
group with no hopeful future, but not everybody took this
pessimistic view. Indeed, there grew a body of opinion that
believed that sometime in the future the working class would
be wealthy, would own industry. and would enjoy political
power. Among the people who argued thus were the socialists.

Claude de Saint-Simon,
socialist writer.

Early Forms of Socialism

Early nineteenth century socialism is difficult to describe both
briefly and accurately, for its supporters held a wide variety of
ideas. Nevertheless, the vast majority accepted the following
argument: the working class must be released from economic
exploitation by the middle classes, especially the owners of
industry; in order to do this, the spirit of cut-throat competition
in commerce and industry must be replaced by one of co-
operation, workers must be released from enslavement by the
machine, they must themselves run industry, and the wealth
of capitalists must be handed over to them. In other words,
socialists believed that the plight of the working class could
not be improved basically merely by such measures as higher
wages and shorter hours of work; instead there must be a completely new economic system.

The strike of the silk workers at Lyon, in November 1831, was suppressed by force.

Socialists also maintained that no existing government would introduce such far-reaching reforms as those just outlined. Therefore the only answer was for the working class itself to take control of the state and then introduce these measures. Socialists were not in agreement as to how the working class could take over government. Some writers, such as Jean Say in France, thought that socialism would simply evolve, and that through natural political development the workers eventually would control government. Others thought that the workers must seize government by revolution; Louis Blanc (who played a prominent part in the revolution of 1848 in France) and Claude de Saint-Simon were of this type.

Socialist views were spread through a variety of means, including the press. In France *The Workers' Journal, The Artisan,* and *The People* were important journals expressing socialist opinions, as was *The Rhineland Gazette* in Germany. Even so, it is doubtful whether early socialism made much impact on workers themselves; it made a stronger appeal to middle class idealists. It is impossible to pick out a precise date when workers began to look to socialism, but it can be said that after the famous strike by silk workers in Lyon in 1831, a strike that was suppressed by force, the European working class increasingly regarded the owners of industry as enemies, and looked to socialism for help.

It has been pointed out that the theories of early socialism took many forms. They were brought together and expressed in their most influential form by Karl Marx.

Karl Marx (1818–83)

Karl Marx was a German Jew (when he was young, his parents were converted to Christianity), and one of the geniuses of the nineteenth century. He was the greatest socialist thinker of all time, and his writings were devoted to the changing of society. Many of his economic, philosophical and political ideas were not new; he was, for example, strongly influenced by Hegel and by the English legal writer, Jeremy Bentham.

After receiving a doctorate from Jena university in 1841 he took up journalism, and then moved to Paris where he spent a great deal of time with French socialists. He also formed a friendship, which lasted for the rest of his life, with Friedrich Engels, a businessman from England, who supported Marx financially for many years.

In 1848 he returned to Germany but was expelled in 1849. He went to London, where he spent most of his time until his death. He lived in poverty, relying mainly on Engels for support, and devoted himself to his writing.

Marx's Theories

Marx published a great deal, but his most famous works are *The Communist Manifesto* (1848) and *Das Kapital* (3 volumes, 1867, 1885, 1894). In these works he argued that history is the story of class warfare. One class dominates society; it exploits lower classes, who must eventually overthrow the ruling class if they are to be free from its control. The way to understand history, he believed, is to see society as being in a state of constant change as one class seeks to overthrow another.

He had to say, of course, why one particular class controls others, and what enables a lower class to come to the top. He found the answer in economics. Whichever class controls the economic life of the state inevitably controls its political life. In other words the ruling class is also the wealthiest. Marx stressed, however, that economic life changes and that new forms of wealth appear, which are in the hands of a new class. The ruling class, afraid that it will be overthrown, tries to keep down its rivals by passing oppressive laws. It cannot hold back the new wealthy class for ever and eventually loses its supremacy. Thus a new ruling class emerges.

Marx illustrated his theory by looking at the past. In the middle ages wealth was based on land, and the more land a person owned the richer he was. Society therefore was dominated by the landowning classes, which consisted of the king, the aristocracy and the bishops (acting for the Church). The growth of trade and industry from the sixteenth to the nineteenth centuries, however, created a new form of wealth, namely capital (such things as money, shipping, factories, mines and machinery). It also created a new class, the middle class (or *bourgeoisie*), which controlled capital. The middle class overthrew the *ancien régime*, as for example in the French Revolution, and established its political control over society.

Marx was convinced that in his own day the supremacy of the *bourgeoisie* was being challenged by a class that arose out of the Industrial Revolution. This was the workers, or *proletariat*.

Friedrich Engels (1820–95). He was born in Germany but from 1849 to 1869 he worked in his father's textiles firm in Manchester after which he concentrated on political work; he collaborated with Karl Marx from 1844 onwards and wrote a great deal in support of Marx.

Karl Marx (1818–83).

Cheap Dress Shop, a cartoon by Cruikshank shows workers being ground down to produce goods and profits.

The workers' form of wealth was their ability to produce goods (Marx called this their 'labour'). He saw their struggle against industrial exploitation by capitalists, and maintained that they would overthrow the *bourgeoisie* and take over the economic and political life of the state. At this point the historical process would stop. When the proletariat took over the state and wiped out remnants of the bourgeois era (Marx called this the 'dictatorship of the proletariat'), there would be no more classes, no more class struggles, no more exploitation and no more revolution.

Marx did not explain why the laws of history should end in this way, but he did not feel that he had to do so. As was said earlier, he wrote in order to change society, not for academics. Many of his ideas were standard nineteenth century socialist theory which now look old-fashioned. His great contribution was to stress that history is about change in society, and to predict the course that the future inevitably would follow. He has made a wider impact on the twentieth century than any other man, for nearly half the world now seeks to organise itself on a Marxist pattern. Doubtless Marx would be horrified at some of the practices carried out in his name, but this applies to every great figure.

Things to Do

1. Imagine you work in a nineteenth century factory; write an account of your work.
2. Study the life of Karl Marx. How accurate do you think that his interpretation of his own age was?
3. Visit any nineteenth century buildings in your area. Find out what materials were used in their construction.
4. Find out how the food and clothing of ordinary people were affected by the Industrial Revolution.

Books to Read or Consult

E. H. Carr, *Studies in Revolution,* London 1962.

E. J. Hobsbawm, *The Age of Revolution, 1789-1848,* London 1965.

K. Marx, *The Communist Manifesto,* ed. A. J. P. Taylor, London 1967.

E. R. Pike, *Human Documents of the Victorian Golden Age,* London 1967.

Lord Shaftesbury (1801–85).

Reform in England, 1815–48

England led the Industrial Revolution and experienced the social problems which accompanied it. Attempts, such as those that follow, were made to cope with these problems.

The Factory Acts

Early in the nineteenth century legislation on conditions of work in industry was rare. The first step was the Factory Act of 1802 by which paupers in cotton mills were to work a maximum of twelve hours a day, and were to do no night work. The scope of this Bill was limited, for it did not cover children whose parents sent them to work, it applied only to cotton mills, and there were no means to enforce it. In fact it was largely ignored, a fate which befell the Factory Acts of 1819 and 1825; they forbade the employment of children under nine in cotton mills, gave children a nine hour day on Saturdays, and extended the twelve hours per day maximum to eighteen-year-olds.

Meanwhile a body of public opinion was growing which urged the government to take a more active concern in conditions of industrial labourers. One of the leaders in this struggle was Antony Ashley Cooper, lord Shaftesbury, (1801–85); every Factory Act was to a greater or lesser extent the outcome of his agitation. A Commission of Inquiry into factory conditions was appointed by the government, and it led to the Factory Act of 1833: the law on child labour in cotton mills was extended to

To poverty-stricken workers looking for relief in this 1830 picture the beadle answers 'My good voman vot should you have children for—don't you know there's no more hoperatives never vanted'. From a factory window the employer claims 'Alas my friends did my Machinery eat & drink I could not employ even that'. From his home *Engine Hall* beside the factory one of his steam carriages comes out while another drives through the unemployed carrying a banner saying 'We want Employment' on the right.

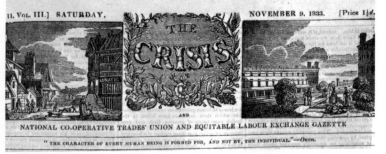

II. Vol. III.] SATURDAY,   THE CRISIS   NOVEMBER 9, 1833.   [Price 1½d.

NATIONAL CO-OPERATIVE TRADES' UNION AND EQUITABLE LABOUR EXCHANGE GAZETTE

"THE CHARACTER OF EVERY HUMAN BEING IS FORMED FOR, AND NOT BY, THE INDIVIDUAL."—*Owen.*

The heading of Robert Owen's periodical *The Crisis*. The pictu compare the life of workers in industrial town and in New Lan

the woollen and linen industries, working children had to attend school for two hours a day, and four inspectors were appointed to enforce the act. While this was an improvement on earlier Acts, Shaftesbury and others continued to campaign for restrictions on the hours that adults (especially women) worked. The going was hard, and it was not until 1847 that the Ten Hours Act was passed, imposing a maximum of ten hours a day in factories for children under eighteen and for all women.

Acts such as these slowly improved the lot of industrial workers, while legislation in 1860, 1864 and 1867 classed more and more industrial enterprises as 'factories', therefore applying the Factory Acts to a greater percentage of the working population.

Early Trades Unions and Robert Owen (1771–1858)

In the early nineteenth century attempts were made by workers themselves to improve their condition. One method was through the formation of trades unions, which became legal in 1824. Many were established between 1824 and 1835, one of the most famous being the Grand National Consolidated Trades Union, founded in 1834 by Robert Owen.

Robert Owen held the exceptional view that factory owners could treat their workers well and at the same time keep profits high. In 1797 he bought a cotton mill at New Lanark in Scotland and put his ideas into practice. They were a success. He was able to introduce education, health programmes, and above-average wages for his workers, and also make a substantial profit.

He formed his Grand National Union with about 500,000 members from different parts of the country, and through it he tried to organise a general strike for an eight hours working day, but the attempt failed badly. This failure damaged the union movement as a whole, and forced Owen to disband the Grand National Union in October 1834, only seven months after its formation.

Another blow was struck at the unions by the law court's decision over some agricultural labourers in Dorset who tried to

A protest march by the Matchmakers Union.

form a union to link up with Owen's union. Membership involved taking an oath. They were prosecuted in 1834 on the grounds that their oath was unlawful, and they were sentenced to seven years transportation. There were demonstrations in support of the 'Tolpuddle martyrs', whose sentences were lifted after two years. Even so, the courts had shown their hostility to the unions and became an obstacle to their development.

Chartism

Another form of worker self-help was Chartism, which demanded not only industrial reforms, but a new system of government sympathetic to the needs of industrial workers. It was led in London by William Lovett, who in 1838 with Francis Place drew up a 'People's Charter' proposing political reforms: universal male suffrage, equal electoral districts, the removal of property qualifications from Members of Parliament, secret ballots, and annual general elections.

Support for the Chartists came to a large extent from people whose position was declining as the Industrial Revolution progressed, such as handloom weavers. Outside of London, Chartism was joined by radical elements; examples are the Birmingham Political Union led by Thomas Attwood, and the Irishman Feargus O'Connor who owned a Leeds newspaper, the *Morning Star*, which became the official organ of the Chartists. In Birmingham, Leeds and elsewhere, marches, demonstrations

The Six Points

OF THE

PEOPLE'S

CHARTER.

1. A VOTE for every man twenty-one years of age, of sound mind, and not undergoing punishment for crime.

2. THE BALLOT.—To protect the elector in the exercise of his vote.

3. NO PROPERTY QUALIFICATION for Members of Parliament—thus enabling the constituencies to return the man of their choice, be he rich or poor.

4. PAYMENT OF MEMBERS, thus enabling an honest tradesman, working man, or other person, to serve a constituency, when taken from his business to attend to the interests of the country.

5. EQUAL CONSTITUENCIES, securing the same amount of representation for the same number of electors, instead of allowing small constituencies to swamp the votes of large ones.

6. ANNUAL PARLIAMENTS, thus presenting the most effectual check to bribery and intimidation, since though a constituency might be bought once in seven years (even with the ballot), no purse could buy a constituency (under a system of universal suffrage) in each ensuing twelvemonth; and since members, when elected for a year only, would not be able to defy and betray their constituents as now.

Subjoined are the names of the gentlemen who embodied these principles into the document called the "People's Charter," at an influential meeting held at the British Coffee House, London, on the 7th of June, 1837:—

Daniel O'Connell, Esq., M.P.,	Mr. Henry Hetherington.
John Arthur Roebuck, Esq., M.P.	Mr. John Cleave.
John Temple Leader, Esq., M.P.	Mr. James Watson.
Charles Hindley, Esq., M.P.,	Mr. Richard Moore.
Thomas Perronet Thompson, Esq., M.P.	Mr. William Lovett.
William Sharman Crawford, Esq., M.P.	Mr. Henry Vincent.

W. COLLINS, PRINTER, "WEEKLY TIMES" OFFICE, DUDLEY.

The Six Points of the People's Charter. One of those involved in preparing the *People's Charter* was Daniel O'Connell, the Irish politician.

96

and meetings were organised in support of the People's Charter. Many London Chartists looked on these developments with suspicion, for they seemed to stand for revolution rather than reform.

In 1839 the Chartists organised a National Convention in London and presented to Parliament a huge petition supporting the Charter. It was turned down and the Convention moved to Birmingham where it was involved in rioting. During the 1840s Chartism increasingly fell under the control of extremists, especially O'Connor, and lost the sympathy of moderates. More petitions were organised, but included too many forged signatures to be taken seriously. Chartism simply died out, but it stands as the first worker movement to last a lengthy period of time.

The Co-operative Movement

A different aspect of early worker self-aid is provided by the co-operative movement. The first successful co-operative was started by some weavers at Rochdale in 1844, who pooled their funds (which came to only £28) and opened a small store which sold goods to members. The scheme was a success, and by 1854 membership had risen from twenty-four to 1,400 and capital had risen to £11,000. Inspired by this example other co-operatives grew, and with them the practice of paying an annual dividend to members on the basis of the amount of goods bought during the year.

Elementary Education

An acute problem in England was the lack of adequate elementary education. An attempt was made to bring education to the poor through the British and Foreign Society (founded in 1807) and the National Society (founded in 1811). To overcome the shortage of teachers, these schools used the monitorial system by which the elder children helped to control the school and to teach the younger children. The two societies spread rapidly, and the National Society, for example, had 500,000 children in its associated schools by 1834.

Finance was a major difficulty, but in 1833 Parliament gave the first state educational grant of £20,000 to the two societies. The grant was increased annually, and in 1839 was put into the hands of a Committee of Council for Education which directed how it should be spent. Another step towards state control of elementary education came in 1840 when school inspectors were appointed.

Although the number of children in primary schools continued to grow, a commission reported in 1861 that the quality of

A school run on the monitorial
system. The teacher first taught a
lesson to the older pupils who,
as monitors, passed it on to the
younger children.

teaching was generally low, and that in order to improve it more
money must come both from the state and from local authorities.
The report also said that funds should be given to schools on
merit, which would be judged by the performance of pupils in
public examinations run by local education boards.

Although measures such as these were a welcome development, problems remained. In districts that were poor, or apathetic
towards education, it was difficult to raise schools to a standard
high enough to earn public money. The answer came with the

A French school for young
children, around 1830.

cabinet maker and his helper,
~~o~~ut of work in 1830, claim that
~~th~~ey have not got enough to
~~li~~ve on.

Education Act of 1870; the country was to be divided into
school districts, the condition of every school was to be
studied, school boards were to be elected to reform inferior
schools, and improvements were to be paid for out of the public
purse. This Act fully established state responsibility for elementary education, laid down certain standards which all schools
had to meet, and put the elementary schools on a sound financial
footing.

The Poor Law

Another social problem concerned the unemployed, the poor
and the aged. Each parish was responsible for helping its poor.
One of the most common ways of doing this in southern
England was the Speenhamland System established in 1795,
by which the income of the poor was supplemented by grants
from the public rates. Although this system saved the poor from
starvation, it put a heavy burden on the ratepayers, while farmers

The unions of parishes set up workhouses. This picture shows the coffin-like beds in the new ward for the poor at Marylebone Workhouse, London 1867.

The verse under this drawing, called *The Sailor's Return or British Valor Rewarded*, reads
> Some, for hard Masters broken under Arms,
> In battle lopt away, with half their Limbs
> Beg bitter bread, thro' realms their Valor sav'd.

tried to save money by keeping the wages of their labourers as low as possible, knowing that they would be helped by the public rates.

A royal commission was appointed to study poor relief and produced its report in 1834, as a result of which the Poor Law Amendment Act was passed in the same year: three commissioners were to be appointed to oversee local authorities in the administration of poor relief; the country was to be divided into unions of parishes which would control relief; the unions were to be run by elected boards of guardians aided by Justices of the Peace. Poor relief was now distributed through new and more effective machinery.

Public Health

Parliament grew concerned over the nation's health. State registers of births, marriages and deaths were established in 1836. The records of deaths included the reason why a person died, and it became clear from them that the health of the nation was in a lamentable condition. Furthermore, commission reports such as that on the *Sanitary Condition of the Labouring Poor* (1842) and those of the Commission on the Health of Large

It seems that French children didn't like being vaccinated or innoculated either.

Towns (1845–7), and the Commission on the Health of the Metropolis (1847–8), produced a horrifying picture of ill-health caused by foul sanitary conditions. They all stressed the need for such things as sewers, flush-lavatories, adequate water supplies, and a central authority to direct sanitary improvements throughout the country.

In the 1840s Parliament took measures such as the acts of 1840 and 1841 which offered free vaccination, and the Public Health Act of 1848 which set up both a general board of health and local boards of health to introduce sanitary improvements. The great cholera epidemic of 1848 drove home the point that unless reforms went ahead on a large scale, disease would run rampant.

An anti-vaccination cartoon showing babies being swallowed by a cow-like creature.

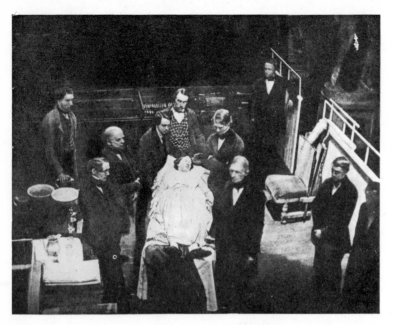

Joseph Lister (1827–1912). In th
mid-1860s, influenced by Pasteu
ideas, experimented with a
carbolic solution to reduce the
danger of infection in operations.

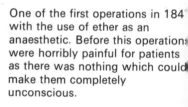

One of the first operations in 184
with the use of ether as an
anaesthetic. Before this operation
were horribly painful for patients
as there was nothing which could
make them completely
unconscious.

Louis Pasteur (1822–95). A
French chemist and micro-
biologist, and one of the greatest
scientists of the nineteenth
century; he showed the connection
between germs and disease, and
developed vaccines for rabies,
anthrax and chicken cholera; the
process whereby milk is
pasteurised is named after him.

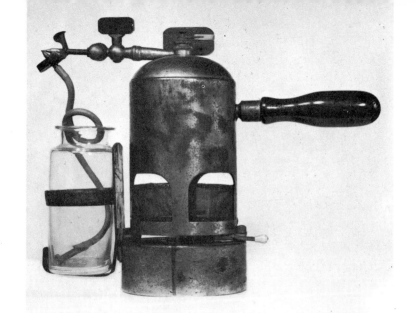

The Lister carbolic spray. This sprayed a solution of carbolic acid on the surgeon's hands and instruments and around the patient during the operation. The patient's wound was also cleaned with the solution. This helped to reduce infection and reduced the number of deaths in operations.

Political Reform

It is clear from the foregoing pages that the state was now responsible for a far wider range of affairs than ever before, and by the end of the 1840s was dealing with social as well as political problems. A favourite method of investigating and finding solutions to problems was the use of commissions, some of which have been mentioned, whose reports (known as 'Blue Books') served as an excellent guide to Parliament.

Reform affected even Parliament itself. After 1815 it was still dominated by landowners. Many of the growing towns were under-represented, and many rural constituencies over-

In 1819 a reform meeting of about 50,000 in St. Peter Fields in Manchester was charged by mounted yeomanry. Eleven people were killed and about four hundred wounded. This was known as the 'Peterloo Massacre'.

represented. This situation was partially changed by the Reform Bill of 1832. Voting qualifications were altered by lowering the required value of property of voters, and the electorate thus rose from 435,000 to 650,000. Of greater importance was the fact that fifty-six 'rotten boroughs' (as the over-represented constituencies were known) completely lost their representation in Parliament, while another thirty lost one of their two Members of Parliament. These seats were given to expanding towns like Sheffield, Leeds and Birmingham, as well as to some of the counties. The reform of 1832 did not turn Britain into a democracy. Even so, it marked the end of the domination of Parliament by small agricultural communities, and saw more prominence given to towns and to the middle classes.

NB

he secret ballot was not intro-
uced until 1872. In this picture of
pen voting we see a cripple,
madman, a prisoner in chains
nd a dying man being brought to
ote in an eighteenth-century
lection.

Things to Do

1. Read about lord Shaftesbury and make a list of his major achievements.
2. Examine the history of trades unions in more detail. How did their development in Ireland compare with that in England?
3. Examine your own school, its buildings, the way that it is run, the subjects that are taught and methods of teaching. Compare these with nineteenth century schools.
4. Find out more about the Reform Bill of 1832. Imagine you are a newspaper reporter, and write an account of a debate between two Members of Parliament, one in favour of the Bill and the other against it.

Books to Read or Consult

G. Kitson Clark, *The Making of Victorian England,* London 1962.

A. Robertson, *The Trade Unions,* London 1965.

D. Thomson, *England in the Nineteenth Century,* London, 1950.

E. L. Woodward, *The Age of Reform, 1815-70,* 2nd ed., Oxford 1962.

Political Problems after 1815

Introduction

In 1815 monarchs were restored to many European states. Some, like Louis XVIII of France, accepted a constitution. Others, such as Ferdinand VII of Spain and Ferdinand IV of the Two Sicilies, introduced oppressive personal rule that forced their subjects into revolution again. In 1820 revolutions occurred in Spain, the Two Sicilies, and Portugal. Spain's problems were made worse by the fact that since 1810 her South American colonies had been in revolt. By 1822 Venezuela, Paraguay, Mexico, Argentine, Colombia, Chile, Peru and San Domingo all became independent; also in 1822 Brazil declared her independence of Portugal.

There was political unrest in Germany too, but it was suppressed by Metternich, the Austrian chief minister, who in 1819 announced the Carlsbad Decrees. The Decrees, which affected most of Germany, established strict censorship of the press, put the universities under state supervision, banned political meetings, and set up commissions to root out secret societies. Since the forces of revolution in Europe were obviously not dead, the forces of conservatism organised against them.

Metternich and Alexander I

Conservatism was dominated by two men; Metternich and Alexander I of Russia. Prince Metternich (1773–1859) became Austrian foreign minister in 1809, and it was he who presided over the Congress of Vienna. Thereafter he devoted himself to the maintenance of the 1815 settlement, which he thought would ensure order and stability within Europe. He recognised, however, that if Europe were to remain stable there must be some capable authority to preserve the 1815 settlement. He saw the answer in strong monarchy, a view similar to that of the eighteenth century *philosophes* who placed their hopes in enlightened kings. Metternich hoped that monarchs would not only uphold order within their states, but would work together for international peace. He even argued that if revolution broke out in one country, then the governments of others were justified in intervening to restore law and order.

Alexander I (1778–1825) also desired a stable Europe, partly for religious reasons. He believed that he had a divine mission to preserve Christian civilisation in Europe, and was convinced that one way to fulfil this mission was to support the 1815 settlement. He therefore lent his aid to the conservatism of Metternich.

Simón Bolívar (1783–1830). The liberator of South America; he studied in Europe and was an admirer of Napoleon; he returned to South America in 1807 determined to free it from Spanish rule; he took a leading part in independence movements there, became president of Peru and Colombia, helped to write a constitution for Bolivia (that was named after him), and wanted to set up a league of South American states; civil war broke out in the new states, and before he died he regretted much of what he had achieved.

Alexander I (1777–1825). A complex character who was part mystic part rationalist, and part liberal part authoritarian; he became tsar in 1801 and was attracted by foreign affairs where he saw a chance to become famous; the fall of Moscow to Napoleon deeply shocked him and pushed him further into mysticism; the Holy Alliance was his idea, and his growing fear of liberalism led him to support Metternich's conservatism.

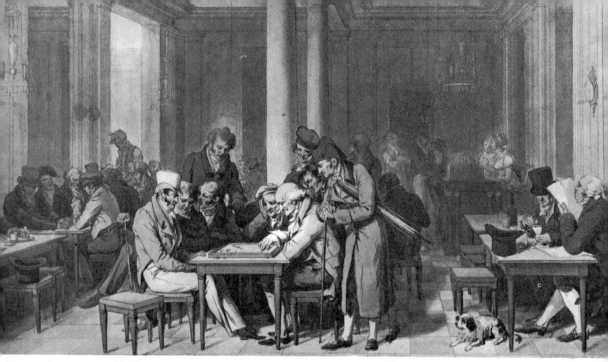

A nineteenth century café where, as well as drinking and playing games, men discussed their political ideas.

Clemens Wenzel Nepomuk Lothar von Metternich (1773–1859). Foreign minister of Austria in 1809 and chancellor in 1821; he was the leading conservative in European politics and consistently opposed liberalism and nationalism; when the revolutions of 1848 broke out he fled to England; although he returned to Austria in 1851 he took no further part in politics.

growing progress & reform & indiv freedom

The Holy Alliance and the Congresses

The basic weapon of conservatism was the Holy Alliance, whose members claimed to uphold Christian principles throughout Europe. It was proposed by Alexander I in 1815, first joined by Russia, Austria and Prussia, and later by most of the states of Europe; Britain, however, refused to join, and Foreign Secretary Castlereagh called the alliance, 'a piece of sublime mysticism and nonsense'. In practice, Christian principles and the 1815 settlement were seen as the same thing, and Metternich was able to use the alliance to his own ends.

The Holy Alliance exerted its influence on a number of international congresses held between 1818 and 1822 to discuss various European problems. The result of the alliance's pressure was that Russia, Austria and Prussia issued the Protocol of Troppau in 1820, which stated that the great powers had the right to crush revolution in other states. Britain rejected the Protocol; nevertheless, on its basis the Austrians were given the task of putting down the revolutions in Italy in 1821, and the French suppressed the Spanish Revolution in 1823.

The forces of conservatism were formidable, and had the backing of three of the most powerful states in Europe. Nevertheless, demands for political change were growing, demands which often regarded the 1815 settlement as an obstacle to progress, and which gathered under two banners; liberalism and nationalism.

Liberalism

Liberalism was a movement that sought many of the benefits that the great Revolution had established in France in the Constitution of 1791. For example, it wanted a constitution, and a representative assembly through which the people could exercise their sovereignty. On the other hand, liberals looked back with horror on the Jacobin period of the French Revolution, and opposed the idea of political power in the hands of the masses. Thus they wanted the vote for propertied people only, so that the lower classes would be excluded from political affairs. To conservative governments liberalism was a revolutionary movement, but to the lower classes it was a conservative one.

The supporters of liberalism came from mixed backgrounds. Some were intellectuals. Many were aristocrats, especially in Italy, Poland and Hungary, where the nobles were losing their traditional leadership of society and wanted to win it back. The wealthiest of the middle classes also generally were liberals, for liberalism promised them political power, put them on a par with many aristocrats, and advocated their superiority over the masses. Below these groups liberalism found few active supporters since it held out little to the lower classes.

Johann Gottlieb Fichte (1762–1814) in the uniform of a Berlin Home Guard.

Nationalism

Nationalism, which began as a reaction against Napoleon's empire, saw a close link between the nation and the state. Its view of the nation was much influenced by the romantic movement in the arts. Romanticism rejected the rationalism of the Enlightenment, and stressed instead the emotions and imagination. This affected the way in which romantics saw the past, which they usually described in idealistic terms; the novels of Sir Walter Scott are a good example. Nationalists similarly often viewed the history of their nation in an idealistic fashion, and sometimes attributed to its people special characteristics. Early German nationalism is a case in point.

Georg Wilhelm Hegel (1770–1831).

Early German Nationalism

The main themes of German nationalism were developed by the writings of two men in particular: Johann Gottlieb Fichte (1762–1814) and Georg Wilhelm Hegel (1770–1831). Fichte had a romantic view of German history (he saw Luther, for instance, as a champion of individual liberty against oppressive authority), which led him to conclude that Germans had a character that fitted them to spread liberty and civilisation throughout Europe. Furthermore, he believed that it was their destiny to do this. Hegel developed a view of the state in which

Giuseppe Mazzini (1805–72).

he saw the state as the instrument through which the German nation could fulfil the task outlined by Fichte; the state was to be a means of national action. Early German nationalism thus was characterised by a romantic view of the past, the conviction that Germans had special qualities, and that they had a historic role to play.

Early Italian Nationalism

In its early stages Italian nationalism differed from German nationalism in that it was less romantic, it claimed few special characteristics for the Italians, and it produced no grand state theory. If any single person expressed its basic features, he was Giuseppe Mazzini (1805–72), who founded the 'Young Italy' movement in 1832. Mazzini believed that the history of mankind was one of progress, and at any one time a single nation has the task of leading the way ahead. The French had recently been the heralds of progress through their great Revolution which had established individual liberty. Now, however, man must take another step along the road of progress; free from the shackles of the past, he needed a goal at which to aim. Mazzini argued that it was the task of the Italian nation both to point out the goal and to lead the way towards it. The goal was a just society based on the nation, a society where individual liberty would be used for the welfare of the nation.

The French Revolution, 1830, and its Effects

In spite of the growth of liberal and national movements, conservatism was far more powerful than revolution in the 1820s. The first successful liberal revolution occurred in France in 1830.

Louis XVIII died in 1824. His successor, Charles X, was a staunch conservative who increasingly opposed the constitution. Matters came to a head on 24 July 1830 when he tried to dismiss the Chamber of Deputies (the Parliament), and alter voting qualifications so that only a conservative Chamber could be elected in future. Protests broke out all over the country, riots spread in Paris, and demands for Charles' overthrow grew. Charles made little attempt to defend himself, and on 2 August abdicated; the duc d'Orléans was elected king and swore to obey a new constitution which put sovereignty in the hands of the people, and which kept the vote in the hands of property owners.

The successful revolution in France encouraged liberal and national movements elsewhere. On I November 1830 a Belgian Congress voted to exclude the Dutch royal family from the Belgian throne. The next year war opened as the Dutch tried to maintain the union with Belgium by force. The great powers

Charles X.

recognised Belgian independence, but Holland did not do so until December 1832. Belgian independence was finally settled in 1839 when the last territorial arrangements between Holland and Belgium were agreed.

A street barricade in Paris, 1 August 1830.

The French Revolution also encouraged revolution in the papal states in 1830. For a time the revolution prospered, but in 1832 Austrian troops intervened, suppressed the revolution, and remained in occupation until 1838.

The Revolutions of 1848 NB

In this chapter it has so far been shown that there were serious political problems in Europe after 1815, as well as the economic and social ones discussed in earlier chapters. In the mid-1840s an economic crisis hit Europe when there was a series of disastrous harvests that led to food shortages, high food prices and unemployment. Although most other parts of Europe did not suffer famine on the same scale as Ireland, there was nevertheless widespread distress. The result was an explosion of revolutions in 1848 in every major country except Britain (including Ireland, which remained peaceful), Russia and Belgium. The first revolt occurred in Sicily in January, but it was the example of the French Revolution in February that sparked off the revolutions elsewhere.

The duc d'Orléans (Philippe Égalité), father of Louis Philippe.

The revolutions were not planned, not the work of professional revolutionaries; people simply rose in rebellion to reject existing conditions. The urban masses demanded work and food; liberals sought liberal constitutions; nationalists hoped for the triumph of nationalism. The revolutions all occurred in towns, especially large ones, for every town with a population over 100,000 rebelled in 1848.

In Germany nationalism was prominent in the revolutions. In May 1848 an assembly of revolutionaries representing the

Paris, the revolution of 1848.

whole of Germany met at Frankfurt to discuss the future of the German nation. Most delegates wanted to unite Germany, but disagreed over its frontiers. Some favoured the 'little Germany' idea of a united Germany that included only Germans, by which they meant people who spoke German; the emphasis was on language, not politics. Others desired a 'greater Germany' that would include the whole of the Austrian empire, with its non-German as well as German subjects. In fact the Frankfurt Assembly decided nothing, for the Prussian and Austrian governments denounced it, and it broke up in June 1849.

In Italy the revolutions were fought mainly over local issues. In Lombardy the rebels hoped to expel the Austrians; in Venice they wanted to restore the former glories of the city-state; the Sicilian revolutionaries wanted independence from Naples; in Piedmont the rebels aimed at a liberal constitution.

The Failure of the Revolutions

Although the revolutions were widespread, with one exception they all failed; the exception was France which was declared a republic. One reason for failure was the lack of co-operation between the revolutionaries, whose interests sometimes clashed. The rebels of one country gave no aid to those of another. On this question the attitude of France was vital, for many revolutionaries hoped that she would lead the forces of radical change in Europe once again. During the 1790s France had given help to uprisings in other countries, but the French revolutionaries of 1848 were a different breed; once they gained control, they abandoned revolution.

A French political club in 1848.

The revolutions also failed because they were restricted to the towns. There was no attempt to rouse the peasants (whom townspeople generally despised), with the result that the troubles of 1848 bypassed the largest single class in society. The conservatives were more shrewd, for they understood that whoever was supported by the peasants would win. The Austrian government, for instance, gained the support of the peasants by abolishing the last few feudal dues that they had to pay; the government in Hungary (part of the Austrian empire) did the same. The result was that throughout the Habsburg dominions the peasants remained peaceful in 1848.

A street barricade in Vienna, 1848.

Russia, too, played a crucial role in the defeat of the revolutions. While the revolutionaries received no support from France, the Austrian and Prussian governments were offered military help by the tsar. This doomed the revolutions in those two states to failure. The Austrian government accepted help, and when the Hungarian rebels were finally crushed in 1849 a Russian army played a major part in their defeat.

Although most of the 1815 settlement survived 1848, it was again challenged in the 1850s and 1860s, in Italy and Germany.

The Unification of Italy

Since 1815 almost the whole of Italy had been under the direct or indirect control of Austria. The only fully independent state was Piedmont-Sardinia, which acted as a refuge for nationalists in exile from other parts of the country. For Italian nationalists the way ahead was clear; Austria must be expelled and Sardinia must lead the struggle. When, however, they turned to the question of the future of Italy, they held differing views. Some, such as Mazzini and Garibaldi (1807–82) dreamed of a united Italy; count Cavour was less enthusiastic. Cavour (1810–61) was prime minister of Piedmont-Sardinia from 1852 until his death, except for a few months in 1859. He pursued the well-being of Sardinia rather than that of Italy. Indeed, the ironic thing is that while he made the greatest single contribution to the unification of Italy, he doubted the benefits of unity and was suspicious of nationalism. His attitude to nationalism is especially interesting. He thought it too inward-looking and liable to isolate Italy from outside economic, political and cultural influences. His own belief was that no country could exist apart from every other and expect to prosper; the more contacts a country had with others the better, and the richer would be the life of its inhabitants. Throughout his career he therefore tried to bring Italy into the mainstream of European affairs and prevent her from falling into the hands of narrow nationalists.

Cavour's Policy

Every Italian agreed that Austria must be expelled from Italy. Since, as has been said, circumstances demanded that Sardinia take the lead, the policy of Cavour was of supreme importance. His basic argument was that Sardinia was too weak to combat Austria alone, and must consequently acquire the aid of some other power. He found the answer in France.

In fact, France offered herself rather than was won over by Cavour. After the declaration of the French Republic in 1848, Louis Napoleon (nephew of the great Napoleon) was elected president; in 1851 he drew up a new constitution, and in 1852 was proclaimed emperor Napoleon III. He dreamed of restoring France's primacy in Europe and saw Italy as one area where this could be done. Contact between France and Sardinia came with the Crimean war (1854–6). Sardinia joined the war in 1855 and fought with France and Britain against Russia. She took part in the peace negotiations in Paris in 1856, where Cavour raised the question of Austria's presence in Italy. This was the first time that Cavour brought the Italian question into international politics.

Franco-Sardinian relations took another, decisive, step in 1858. Napoleon III proposed a marriage between his cousin and the daughter of Victor Emmanuel II, king of Piedmont-Sardinia. Cavour met Napoleon at Plombières in July 1858 to discuss both this and the Italian question. Cavour persuaded Napoleon to give help to Sardinia in expelling Austria from Italy; Italy would then be divided into three states, a northern, central, and southern (the northern state to be under the king of Piedmont-Sardinia); France would be rewarded with Nice and Savoy. By this agreement Cavour won the support of France, and Napoleon had the chance to turn France into the most influential power in Italy. The two governments signed an official alliance in January 1859.

Napoleon III (1808–73). Nephew of the great Napoleon, he was elected president of France in 1848 and emperor in 1852; he hoped to restore the glory of France through an ambitious foreign policy; he thus involved France in the Crimean war, in the Italian question, tried to create an empire in Mexico, and hoped to become king of Spain; during the Franco-Prussian war he was captured at Sedan; he was overthrown and went into exile in England, where he died.

The War

Austria was alarmed at Sardinian policy and in April 1859 sent an ultimatum to disarm. Cavour refused, the Austrians invaded, and in May France declared war on Austria.

The part played by French troops decided the issue. In June the Austrians were defeated twice, at Magenta and Solferino. There were revolts elsewhere in Italy, and Tuscany, Parma and Modena declared their independence of Austria and joined Sardinia. All was going well for Cavour; then in July he heard the shattering news that Napoleon had come to terms with the Austrians at Villafranca and had backed out of the war. Napoleon had agreed that Austria would give up Parma and Lombardy to France (who would later grant them to Sardinia, at a price), Modena and Tuscany would be restored to their former rulers, and Austria would retain Venetia.

Furious at the news, Cavour resigned. It is thought that the principal reasons why Napoleon III so quickly abandoned the war were that his regime was weak and facing much opposition at home, and that he feared the outbursts of Italian nationalism that accompanied the war. He was afraid that he was letting loose another series of revolutions which perhaps nobody could control.

Cavour was not yet beaten. He was recalled as prime minister in January 1860 and urged that the future of Parma, Tuscany and Modena be decided on a vote by the electors in those states. Voting took place in March 1860, and all three states decided to join Piedmont-Sardinia. France agreed to the decision in return for Nice and Savoy; Austria had no choice but to assent.

Unification

Although Cavour had acquired these states for Sardinia, Italian nationalists were bitterly disappointed. They saw Napoleon III as a deceiver and were dismayed that Cavour appeared to have little ambition to create a united Italy.

At this point Garibaldi stepped in. He had organised guerrillas to fight the Austrians, and in May 1860 he and 1,000 of his 'Redshirt' supporters set sail for southern Italy to raise nationalist rebellion there. Against all expectations he was successful. He seized Palermo and Naples and then marched towards Rome, which, because of its religious significance, and its status in the ancient Roman empire, was regarded by all Italians as the capital city of any new united Italy.

Cavour, who in September 1860 accompanied Sardinian troops on an invasion of the Papal States, grew alarmed at Garibaldi's success. French troops were quartered in Rome and Cavour feared a quarrel with France if Garibaldi's men

...seppe Garibaldi (1807–82). ...rn in France, he was an ardent ...lian nationalist and republican; ...joined Mazzini's Young Italy ...vement in 1833, but his ...litical activities forced him to ...e; he was in South America ...m 1836 to 1848, when he ...urned to Italy and joined in the ...olutions; although a republican ...met Cavour in 1856 and ...reed to support him against ...stria; his most spectacular ...hievement was the invasion of ...uthern Italy in 1860; he was ...marily a soldier with little ...npathy for politicians or ...rliaments.

Otto von Bismarck (1815–98).

fought them. He therefore marched south to meet Garibaldi to try to come to some agreement over the future of Italy. It was soon clear that Italian unification was going to take place, for in October Naples and Sicily voted for unity with Sardinia. Cavour, Garibaldi and Victor Emmanuel II met, and agreed upon a united kingdom of Italy. In February 1861 an Italian parliament proclaimed Victor Emmanuel king and on 17 March the kingdom of Italy was announced. In fact Italy was not yet fully united, for Venetia, and Rome with its provinces, still remained outside the kingdom. Venetia was acquired in 1866, and Rome in 1870; the major work, however, was done.

The Unification of Germany

Like the unification of Italy, the unification of Germany took place mainly at the expense of Austria. Austria hoped to develop a 'greater Germany', a Germany including several states and nations under the leadership of Vienna. Prussia wanted a 'little Germany' including Germans only, and based on central government from Berlin. The clash between these two approaches was the greatest political issue in Germany from 1848 to 1871.

The 1848 revolutions resulted in a triumph for Austria. During the turmoil Prussia tried to break up the German Confederation

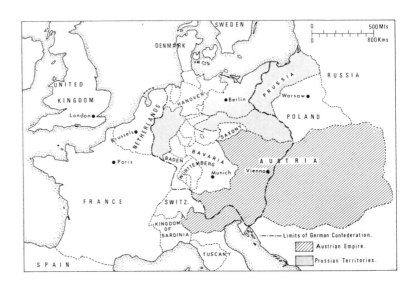

German States before 1866.

set up in 1815, but was foiled by Austria. At an agreement signed at Olmütz in 1850 Prussia gave in and recognised the continuance of the Confederation. This was how matters stood throughout the 1850s. They were changed in the 1860s, mostly because of the achievements of Otto von Bismarck (1815–98).

Bismarck

Bismarck was appointed Prussian premier in 1862. Cavour was his model, and just as Cavour was a servant of Piedmont-Sardinia first and Italy second, so Bismarck was a Prussian first and German second. Some historians say that from the moment he took office Bismarck wanted to unite Germany; others argue that he was an opportunist whose plans grew with circumstances. Whichever is true, Bismarck destroyed Austria's influence in Germany and overthrew France as the most powerful state in western Europe.

The Schleswig-Holstein Question

Bismarck's first international problem concerned Schleswig-Holstein in southern Denmark, an issue over which he had to ally with Austria. In Schleswig-Holstein most people were German, and by a treaty of 1852 the area was given a special position in the Danish constitution. When Christian IX became king of Denmark in 1863, however, he ignored the treaty and brought Schleswig-Holstein fully into the kingdom.

German nationalism was enraged. Saxon and Hanoverian troops marched into Holstein to defend it against Christian. William I of Prussia was also angered and urged Bismarck to declare war on Denmark. Reluctantly Bismarck agreed, and in order that the other European powers would not suspect Prussia of expansionism he signed an alliance with Austria in January 1864. Together their troops invaded Schleswig in February.

In London, in April, at a conference of Britain, Russia, France, Austria and Prussia, Bismarck realised that none of the powers would or could stop Prussia acting alone against Denmark. He therefore dropped the alliance with Austria. The war itself came to an end with the treaty of Vienna in 1864 when Denmark handed Schleswig-Holstein to Prussia and Austria jointly.

Bismarck and Austria

Bismarck now turned to the question of Germany. He wanted Prussia and Austria to divide Germany along the river Main, with Prussia controlling territory to the north, and Austria to the south. To strengthen his position in negotiating with Austria, Bismarck came to terms with France in 1865 and signed an alliance with Italy in 1866.

During 1866, Bismarck tried to reach agreement with Austria, but the Austrians were not willing to divide Germany unless Prussia promised them support in Italy. Bismarck, however, had already committed Prussia to France and Italy and so could reach no agreement with Austria. He felt that he therefore had no option but to enforce his German solution by war with Austria, which he provoked in June 1866.

Austria, faced with attack by Prussia, found herself in a worse position when Italy declared war later in June. Within seven weeks Prussia defeated Austria and peace was signed at Prague in September 1866: Austria was expelled from Germany; the German Confederation of 1815 was dissolved; Prussia annexed Hanover, Hesse, Frankfurt and Nassau; other states north of the Main were to be members of a new North German Confederation under Prussia; the states south of the Main (Bavaria, Baden, Württemberg, and Hesse-Darmstadt) were to be independent. To complete her expansion in 1866 Prussia annexed Schleswig-Holstein in December. Austria's decline continued. Peace was signed between herself and Italy at Vienna in October 1866, when Italy acquired Venetia, Austria's last Italian territory.

Bismarck and France

Relations between France and Prussia had so far been good, but now began to deteriorate. When, for example, Napoleon III tried to buy Luxembourg from Holland in 1867, Bismarck was responsible for calling an international conference which forbade the purchase and so damaged Napoleon's prestige. Bismarck's policies were still centered on Germany; he hoped to bring the south German states under Prussian rule. If possible, he wanted French approval, but was ready to go ahead without it.

In 1868 a chance arose to improve Prussian prestige. There was a revolution in Spain and the Cortes (Parliament) offered the throne to a Hohenzollern prince, Leopold. French public opinion reacted strongly against this, for Prussia had been too successful in recent years for France to feel secure. Leopold, however, turned down the Spanish throne, and so nothing came of the matter. It was re-opened in 1870 when the throne was again offered to Leopold, who this time accepted it. Once again there was an outcry in France, so fierce that Leopold's acceptance was withdrawn. Bismarck was angry. It was clear that if the French were opposed to a potentially pro-Prussian king of Spain, they certainly would resist the more important development of a southern Germany under Prussia.

Although Leopold had declined the Spanish throne, Napoleon III was not satisfied. He sent his ambassador in Berlin to meet William I at Ems, the traditional German royal spa, to demand that Leopold would never again consider the Spanish throne. William refused and sent a telegram to Bismarck informing him of the episode. A shortened version of the telegram appeared in the press, giving the impression that Napoleon III had put an ultimatum to William. Both French and Prussian public opinion was inflamed at the high-handed attitude of the other side; French opinion was so outraged that the government declared war on Prussia on 19 July 1870.

Some historians say that Bismarck wanted a war with France; he therefore encouraged Leopold to take the throne of Spain, and deliberately leaked the Ems telegram to the press, believing that war would follow. Others say that he did not want a war and expected the French government to back down over the Ems telegram; he wanted a victory of prestige over France that would build up Prussia's reputation in southern Germany.

The War

From France's point of view the war was an utter disaster. Defeat followed defeat, the greatest being at Sedan on 1 September 1870; this date later became a national holiday in Germany to celebrate the foundation of the empire. Revolution broke out in Paris, a republic was once more declared, and the military situation continued to grow worse. In September the Prussians reached Paris and besieged the city. There were more defeats for France at Metz, Strasbourg and S. Quentin, and on 28 January 1871 Paris surrendered. Peace was signed at Frankfurt in May 1871: France handed over Alsace-Lorraine

The town of St. Cloud during the Franco-Prussian war.

to Germany (as Prussia had just become); she agreed to pay 5,000 million francs to Germany; she was to be occupied until the sum was paid. These terms created long enmity between the two countries, and good relations were not restored until the 1950s.

Developments in Germany

Bismarck's major purpose still remained to bring the south German states under Prussian control. During the war public opinion throughout Germany rallied to Prussia, and in October 1870 the four south German states met to discuss their future.

Revolution broke out in Paris: the burning of the palace of the Tuileries 1871.

120

William I is proclaimed German emperor, January 1871.

Hesse-Darmstadt and Baden were in favour of joining the North German Confederation, Württemberg wavered, and Bavaria was opposed to the plan. Bismarck moved in and applied pressure, so that in November all four states signed unity agreements with Prussia. Bismarck applied more pressure and persuaded the Bavarian government to invite the Prussian king to become emperor of the united Germany; in January 1871 William I was proclaimed German emperor.

A Comment

Bismarck did not unite the whole of Germany; many Germans remained, for example, in the Austrian empire. The so-called

United Germany 1870.

121

'unification of Germany' was in fact the expansion of Prussia, or the victory of the 'little Germany' idea. The new Germany had a population of about 41 millions: this compared with about 38 millions in France and 31 millions in Britain. She therefore became the most populous state in central and western Europe, as well as the strongest militarily. Furthermore, industrialisation was going ahead, and by the end of the century Germany was to rival Britain. The emergence of this new Germany meant the end of France's hopes of dominating western Europe.

Things to Do

1. Imagine you are a German or Italian nationalist; write an argument in favour of your cause.
2. Take one example of a revolution in 1848, read as much about it as you can and find out to what extent it was the result of local problems as well as general ones.
3. Study the lives of Cavour and Garibaldi. Whom do you think made the greater contribution to Italian unification?
4. Examine Bismarck's domestic policy. What measures did he take to bind Germany together?

Books to Read or Consult

R. Albrecht-Carrié, *A Diplomatic History of Europe since 1815,* London 1966.

E. Kedourie, *Nationalism,* London 1960.

D. Mack Smith, *The Making of Italy, 1796-1866,* London 1968.

J. L. Talmon, *Romanticism and Revolt,* London 1967.

A. J. P. Taylor, *Bismarck,* London 1968.

The Rush for Empires, 1870–1914

Introduction

For most of the nineteenth century European states showed little active interest in their overseas empires. Indeed, much public opinion was opposed to the development of empires. Liberals usually argued that they were economically unprofitable, while socialists saw them as pawns of capitalism. Nevertheless, Europe's control of the outside world grew more and more extensive during the 1800s. Sometimes this took a military form. By 1840 Spain had completed its conquest of the Philippines, by 1870 Holland had subjected Indonesia, and by 1909 France and Britain had partitioned Indo-China, where only Siam remained independent. Another form of intervention was economic, the principal instrument being the trading company. The British East India Company, for example, not only monopolised trade between Britain and India, but also administered large areas of India until the British government took over in 1858.

The Rush for Empires after 1870

From about 1870 there was an astonishing revival as one after another European states set out to create or to extend their empires. Several factors help to explain this phenomenon, although historians are not agreed upon their relative importance.

The Industrial Revolution created a demand for raw materials and for markets where manufactured goods could be sold; colonies could provide both, although this was not always the case. Again, as the European population grew, social and economic tensions forced people to emigrate. From Britain, for example, some 21,500,000 emigrated between 1815 and 1914; it is significant that about 13,500,000 went to the U.S.A. and

rd and lady Curzon with Indian tables in a maharajah's palace.

Feeding time between decks on an emigrant ship, 1872.

only 8,000,000 to the empire. National prestige was also involved in the creation of empires. French national honour needed to be restored by successes abroad to compensate for defeat in the Franco-Prussian war. In Germany demands grew for a repetition in the colonial sphere of the recent climb to supremacy in western Europe. Britain's renewed interest in her empire was based mainly on self-defence. She feared that European rivals wanted to take over the empire, which might collapse unless steps were taken to strengthen it.

The Attraction of China

The continent most attractive to European ambitions was Asia, with its huge population and legendary wealth. India, one of the most valuable jewels in the Asian treasure chest, was controlled by Britain. China, however, was independent. It was a mysterious land with an ancient civilisation, ruled by emperors of the Manchu dynasty. The Chinese looked down on all foreigners as barbarians and kept their contact with the outside world to a minimum. Commerce with Europe had developed in the seventeenth and eighteenth centuries, and the first American merchant ship arrived at Canton in 1784. Foreign traders were restricted to a few ports and to certain areas within these ports.

124

An opium den in China.

A Chinese archer ill-equipped to fight against modern troops.

Rules covering commercial and personal behaviour by foreigners were strict, and were codified by the Chinese government in the Eight Regulations of 1819.

The Opium War, 1839–42

Relations between foreigners and the Chinese were always strained, for each despised the other. During the 1830s the Chinese government increasingly resented the British, who had developed an extensive trade in Indian opium. The government was alarmed at the disastrous effects that opium had on the millions of people who smoked it, and also objected to the money lost through its purchase. In 1839 an attempt was made to stamp out the trade, and fighting broke out with the British. The British government decided that the opium trade was so important to the Indian economy that it must be maintained, and therefore continued the war until the Chinese were forced to sign peace at Nanking in 1842. China was to pay an indemnity to Britain, five ports were opened to British trade (Canton, Amoy, Foochow, Ningpo and Shanghai), and Hong Kong was given to Britain. The war proved how weak China was and how easily concessions could be wrung from its government.

Further Chinese Concessions

Other states learnt the lesson of the war, and in the 1840s forced China to give in to many of their demands. In 1844 Americans gained exemption from Chinese lawcourts, and

The western army takes Peking, October 1860.

France obtained toleration for the Roman Catholic faith. Toleration was extended to Protestantism in 1845. By 1850 Belgium, Norway, Russia and Sweden had all acquired commercial rights. In the ports open to western trade foreign communities built warehouses, churches, schools and hospitals. Local residents detested these intrusions and there was constant ill-will and violence between Chinese and foreign 'barbarians'.

The Wars of 1856–60

Because of permanent tension renewed conflict was never far away. It broke out again in 1856 when a French missionary was executed by the Chinese authorities. French and British fleets carried the war to northern China. After a pause between 1858 and 1859 the war continued, and this time a Franco-British army even captured the capital, Peking (1860). Once more the Chinese government had to accept humiliating terms. Eleven more ports and the Yangtze river were opened to western trade, missionaries were allowed to spread their faith, foreign legations were to be established in Peking, China was to pay another indemnity, and the opium trade was legalised.

Discontent was spreading in China at the extent of foreign influence and at China's defeats in war. The upper classes in particular demanded reforms to strengthen and equip China to expel the foreigners. However, no appreciable progress was made. A worse threat came in the 1890s, the possibility of the partition of the country, and at the head of this new menace was Japan.

Chinese soldiers, like this member of the imperial army, fought bravely against the guns of the western army.

Japan

Like China, Japan had long remained isolated from the west. In the first half of the nineteenth century her society was still feudal in structure. Effective government was in the hands of the *shogun* who resided at Edo (Tokyo). Beneath him were the great landowners (the *daimyos*), whose authority was enforced by professional soldiers (the *samurais*). The emperor (the *mikado*) was primarily a religious leader and resided at Kyoto. Contact with the west was established in 1854 when a commercial treaty was signed with the U.S.A. Other treaties were signed with Britain, Holland and Russia in 1854 and 1855, and another with the U.S.A. in 1856.

In 1868 Mutshuhito became emperor. During his reign (which lasted until 1912) he overthrew the power of the *shogun*, established a strong centralised government based on western patterns, and industrialised the country as rapidly as possible. Under Mutshuhito Japan borrowed increasingly from western political and industrial models and became the first extensively westernised Asian state. Japan also developed imperial ambitions and in the 1890s tried to grab her share of China's wealth.

The Sino-Japanese War, 1894–5

Japan quarrelled with China over Korea, which Japan regarded as independent and which China saw as a vassal state. Japan wanted to supplant China as the main influence there, and in 1894 demanded that the Korean government accept only Japanese troops to put down a revolution that had broken out. During the argument war broke out in July 1894 when some Japanese fired on Chinese warships.

The war was brief. The Chinese were overwhelmed, and the Japanese expelled them from Korea, invaded Manchuria and seized Port Arthur on the Liaotung peninsula. Peking itself was in danger and the Chinese government had to accept Japan's peace terms at Shimonoseki in 1895. Four more ports were opened to Japanese and western trade, China was to pay an indemnity, and she gave Formosa, the Pescadores and the

A section of the 4,000 mile Trans-Siberian railway.

Liaotung peninsula to Japan. The western powers were disturbed at Japan's success and forced her to return the Liaotung peninsula to China. They also followed Japan's example and began to annex Chinese territory. Thus the partition of the 'Celestial Empire' started.

The Partition of China

In 1895 France forced China to grant territory to Annam, which was controlled by France. Two years later China handed over more territory in the south to Britain. In 1898 Germany seized Kiaochow bay where she built the port of Tsingtao. Also in that year Russia leased the Liaotung peninsula and began to fortify Port Arthur. Finally in 1898 Britain leased Weihaiwei and the mainland opposite Hong Kong.

As well as these measures, the western powers built roads and railways in regions that they might take in future. The Russians built a railway from Port Arthur across Manchuria to

A stockyard of the Trans-Siberian railway.

128

Boxer child carries a big knife to be used in driving out the barbarians'.

Christians are represented as goats in this Boxer anti-Christian picture.

link up with the Trans-Siberian railway. Between 1896 and 1900 the French were given permission to build railways in the south-east. In 1899 Germany and Britain acquired the right to construct a railway between Tientsin and the Yangtze; Britain also got permission to build roads from Shanghai to Nanking and from Shanghai to Hangchow.

The Attitude of the U.S.A.

Through her acquisition of Hawaii and the Philippines in 1898 the U.S.A. became firmly committed to affairs in the Pacific. She viewed the partition of China with concern, fearing that the European powers would close their territories to their commercial rivals. The U.S.A. wanted an 'open door' policy whereby the treaty ports would remain open to everybody. In 1899 she proposed this policy to the European powers and Japan. It was accepted, but without enthusiasm and with many exceptions. The U.S.A. remained the only power firmly behind the 'open door' principle.

The Boxer Rising

The foreigners had to sink their rivalry for a while in face of the rising of the Boxers, a secret society dedicated to the expulsion of the 'barbarians'. The Boxers were especially strong in the province of Shantung, and when an economic crisis resulting from heavy floods and bad harvests hit Shantung in 1898, they

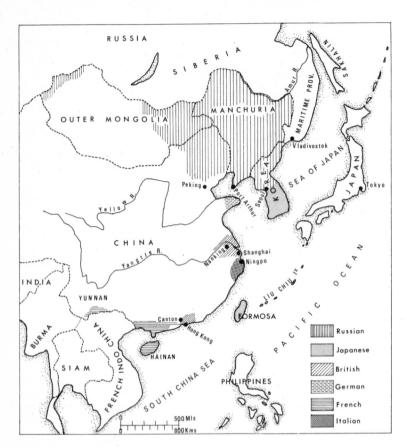

Areas of influence of the great powers in China, about 1900.

The dowager empress Tzu-Hsi.

burst into violence against the hated foreigners and those Chinese who had turned Christian.

The response of the Chinese government was at first in doubt. The young emperor Kuang-hsü tried to introduce westernising reforms in 1898, but was stopped by conservative opposition led by the empress dowager T'zu-hsi. She overthrew the reformers and imprisoned the emperor. Once in control, she lent the government's support to the Boxers.

In Peking the foreign legations prepared to defend themselves against Boxer attack. A European relief force from Tientsin tried to reach them, but failed, and on 20 June 1900 the empress dowager declared war on the foreign states. The Boxers laid siege to the legations in Peking and in Europe vast press coverage was given to their fate. Meanwhile another relief force was gathered which managed to reach Peking and broke into the city and relieved the legations on 14 August 1900.

This saw the beginning of the collapse of the rising. The government fled from Peking, which was pillaged by the foreign troops. Some 45,000 foreign soldiers poured into northern

...inese troops during the Boxer ...ellion.

China and wreaked a terrible revenge, killing and looting where-
ever they went. When the Boxers finally were crushed, the
western powers and Japan haggled over the terms to impose on
the Chinese. Finally they settled on the Boxer Protocol of
September 1901 by which almost one hundred Boxer leaders
were to be punished (ten were executed) and China had to pay
a huge indemnity. Although the Boxer movement failed, it was
the first mass attempt to expel the foreigners. As the century
progressed more attempts were made, success coming when
the Communists led by Mao Tse-tung seized control of the
country in 1949.

...estern soldiers guard the back
...trance to the American legation.

The tsar holds up an icon and blesses troops about to leave for the front, in the Russo-Japanese war.

Russian Expansion and its Consequences

At the turn of the century Russian influence in China began to expand rapidly. In 1900 Russia seized the whole of Manchuria, linked Port Arthur with the Trans-Siberian railway as was stated earlier, and after the Boxer rising put thousands of troops into Manchuria, thus effectively bringing it into the Russian empire.

Japan was deeply offended, for she felt that Port Arthur and the Liaotung peninsula should have been hers at the peace of Shimonoseki. She was further disturbed when Russia extended her influence to Korea and threatened to replace Japan as the most dominant power.

Britain too was alarmed. In her fears for the safety of the empire she regarded Russia as a chief rival in Asia. She feared that Russia wanted to subject central Asia and perhaps even take over India itself. What was worse, Russia was a land power in Asia and therefore was immune from the Royal Navy, which was the main protection of the British empire. Russia's seizure of Manchuria was seen as the first step of a period of Russian expansion.

In 1902 Britain signed an alliance with Japan which was aimed at Russia. The alliance promised to keep the territorial situation in China as it now was. The alliance was renewed in 1905, but this time applied also to India and the whole of east Asia. This was the first time that a European power had signed an alliance with an Asian state on the basis of equality.

The Russo-Japanese War

Although Japan wanted to stem Russian influence in Korea, she was prepared to partition it. She made a proposal to this effect but the Russian government failed to reply. This confirmed

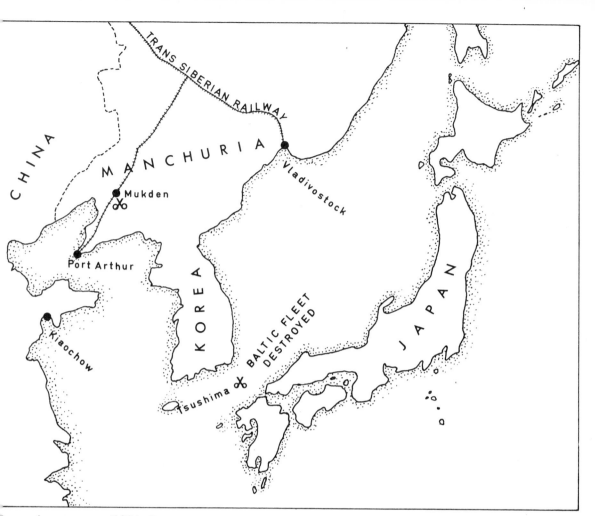

Russo-Japanese war, 1904–5.

the Japanese in their suspicion that Russia was bent on controlling the whole of Korea. In February 1904 Japan broke off diplomatic relations with Russia and war began.

It seemed inevitable that Russia, one of the great powers, should crush Japan. Incredibly the reverse happened. The Japanese captured the Liaotung peninsula, destroyed the Russian Far Eastern fleet, and when the Baltic fleet was sent to the war zone, destroyed it too at the battle of Tsushima straits in May 1905. Seoul in Korea also was captured and the Korean government had to break its links with Russia. President Theodore Roosevelt of the U.S.A. offered to mediate in peace talks. They took place and peace was signed at Portsmouth in the U.S.A. in September 1905. The Liaotung peninsula passed to Japan, but the rest of Manchuria was returned to China.

The effects of the war were profound. Never before had an Asian state defeated a western power. This example encouraged other Asian nations wishing to break the control of Europe. Asian nationalism stems from many sources, but one of the most important is the Russo-Japanese War. The war also proved that since Japan formed part of east Asia, she had a great advantage over the western states; in the long run she, not they, was going to dominate that part of the world.

The Anglo-Russian *Entente*

Russia's defeat eased Britain's fears regarding Asia. Already Britain had discovered that Russia had fewer ambitions than was thought. In 1904 a British expedition had invaded Tibet to prevent her falling into Russian hands. The expedition found, however, that there was no Russian influence in Tibet, nor did Russia desire any.

Russia in fact was in a weak position. A revolution broke out there in 1905, and although it was put down, it proved how fragile was the tsarist regime. The Russian government thus welcomed the idea of settling its differences with Britain. In 1907 an agreement, or *entente*, was reached over all the areas where the two countries were at odds. The main decision concerned Persia; the north became a Russian sphere, the southeast a British sphere, and the rest neutral. 1907 saw the end of Anglo-Russian rivalry.

Africa

Asia is but one area of the world where European states made their impact. Africa is another. The attraction of Africa at first seems difficult to understand. In the mid-nineteenth century it was largely unknown by Europeans, communications there were difficult, the native populations were frequently hostile, and commercially it had much less to offer than Asia. Nevertheless Africa was partitioned by European states (Asian states and the U.S.A. were not involved). Most governments, those of Britain and France for instance, did not want to be drawn into Africa but were carried along by events. The political control that European countries established in Africa was in some cases very much against their will, as will be seen.

The Exploration of Africa

In 1800 Africa south of the Sahara was almost a complete blank on European maps, but by 1900 few areas remained unknown. Almost every west European nation contributed to the exploration of Africa, British explorers playing a distinguished role. Early in the century Mungo Park travelled up the Niger, and in the 1820s Clapperton studied its course. Most famous of all was David Livingstone, who was sent to Africa in 1841

Commercially Africa had less to offer than Asia but some manufacturers saw it as a new market for their products, as this late nineteenth century advertisement shows.

134

The meeting of Stanley and Livingstone, in an African village, 1871

King Leopold II of Belgium.

by the London Missionary Society. After missionary work in Bechuanaland he crossed the Kalahari desert in 1849, explored the Zambezi river in the 1850s, and in the 1860s searched for the source of the Nile in Tanganyika. In this he failed, the honour going to H. M. Stanley, who made his name by finding Livingstone in 1871 when he had been thought lost for several years. After finding Livingstone, Stanley explored the Congo, where he signed commercial treaties with local chiefs on behalf of Leopold II of Belgium (the British government had no interest in such plans). His search for the source of the Nile was rewarded in 1881 when he tracked it to lake Edward.

These are but a few of the explorers, missionaries and traders who gradually opened up Africa. The government of Leopold II was the only one to take an active interest in establishing influence in Africa; other European governments generally ignored developments there. This attitude was to change, however, one of the most important reasons being events in north Africa.

The Egyptian Problem

The opening of the Suez Canal in 1869 had strengthened Egypt's position as the focal point of many trade routes between Europe and Asia. France and Britain carried considerable weight there, and when in 1882 a nationalist rising broke out against the corrupt, inefficient rule of the khedive Tewfik, it was also aimed at the growing power of the English and French financial controllers who 'advised' Tewfik on the administration of his territories.

After some hesitation Britain and France decided to support Tewfik's regime, for its collapse could mean the end of their ascendancy. A British army was therefore sent to aid the khedive and it defeated the rebels at Tel el Kebir in August 1882. The British government wanted to bring the army straight home, but rapidly discovered that Tewfik's authority was so weak that revolution would break out again if the troops were withdrawn. The situation was further complicated when the revolution spread to the Sudan.

The Sudan

The Sudanese rising was led by a Muslim fanatic, Mohammed Ahmed, the *mahdi*. He aimed to destroy Egypt's control of the Sudan and in 1883 wiped out an Egyptian army. British troops were then sent to protect Egypt's southern border. Khartoum fell to the *mahdi* in 1885 after being defended by general Gordon, and for the time being the British contented themselves simply with keeping the frontier secure. In this way Britain reluctantly occupied Egypt.

The French were deeply offended. They felt deceived and thought that Britain had deliberately used the Egyptian problem to oust French influence there. Their former joint position had ended; Egypt was now a British preserve. Hereafter France was Britain's firm rival in Africa. She carved out an empire in west Africa and tried to extend her authority across to the upper Nile. The example set by Britain and France was followed by other states, and so the race to partition Africa set in.

The Spread of Partition

Before the 1880s the governments of Britain and France had a 'gentlemen's agreement' to keep out of west Africa and the Congo (hence Britain's refusal to support Stanley's plan for treaties in the Congo). Foiled in Egypt, the French now began to assert their authority in west Africa. Also in 1876 Leopold II of Belgium founded the International African Association, whose aim was systematically to explore Africa. Leopold's ambition settled on the Congo, for he thought that if he could control it he would become a great ruler of international fame. Portugal already controlled Angola and Mozambique. She hoped also to acquire the Congo and create a vast trans-Africa empire. Germany developed a desire for possessions in Africa mainly for reasons of national prestige. Between 1883 and 1885 she established control over Togoland, the Cameroons, German South-West Africa and German East Africa.

Germany also sought to exploit the Anglo-French disagreement. It will be described later how Bismarck's foreign policy after 1871 aimed to keep France isolated in order to ensure Germany's domination of western Europe. So long as France and Britain were at loggerheads over Africa, there was no

Charles George Gordon (1833–85). Born near London he joined the British army in 1852 and served in China from 1860–4; in 1874 the khedive of Egypt employed him to open up the upper Nile, and in 1877 he became governor-general of the Sudan; he returned to England but was recalled to Egypt when the *mahdi* rebelled and was instructed to try and pacify him; instead Gordon tried to defend Khartoum against the *mahdi*; Khartoum held out for 317 days, but on 26 January 1885 it fell and Gordon was killed.

British troops in Egypt 1882.

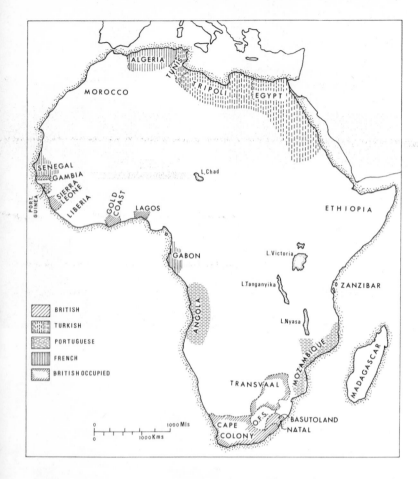

Africa in 1879.

chance of an alliance between them. Bismarck encouraged their dissension by helping France to offset her 'defeat' in Egypt. He supported France in west Africa and in 1884 came to an agreement with her on how their two countries should partition that part of the continent.

The Berlin Congress

There were now enough clashing interests in Africa to present problems to European governments. Bismarck proposed an international conference to discuss the partition of that continent and the avoidance of future quarrels. The congress met in Berlin in 1884 and 1885 and reached a number of agreements. Some areas, such as the river Niger, the Congo basin and east Africa, were to be free trade areas. The Congo Free State was set up under Leopold II. Britain acquired the Niger delta, while France received a number of territories north of the Congo and had her supremacy in west Africa recognised.

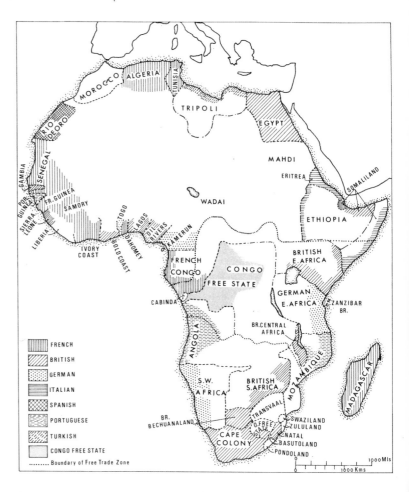

Areas in Africa under European control by 1891.

It was decided that a European government need only establish 'effective occupation' of a part of Africa (although this was not defined) and inform other governments, for that region to be annexed.

The Fashoda Incident

Although Britain held Egypt, she believed that her supremacy would be secure only if she controlled the whole length of the Nile. Since the Nile was crucial to the Egyptian economy, whoever controlled it had Egypt within his grip. To fulfil this plan Britain needed to dominate the Sudan, through which the Nile passed, and between 1896 and 1898 Anglo-Egyptian forces conquered the Sudan and removed Britain's fears.

France resented this development. She hoped to spread her own presence across to the upper Nile so that Egypt should to a certain extent be dependent on France. In 1898 a small French

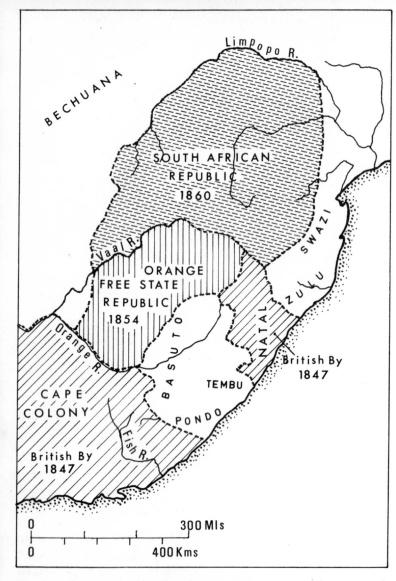

BECHUANA

Limpopo R.

SOUTH AFRICAN
REPUBLIC
1860

Vaal R.

ORANGE
FREE STATE
REPUBLIC
1854

Orange R.

SWAZI

ZULU

NATAL

British By
1847

CAPE
COLONY

British By
1847

Fish R.

BASUTO

TEMBU

PONDO

| 0 | | | 300 MIs |
| 0 | | | 400 Kms |

South Africa in 1860.

force under captain Marchand was sent to occupy the town of Fashoda, which controlled the upper Nile. He arrived in July 1898. In September lord Kitchener, head of the Anglo-Egyptian forces and conqueror of the Sudan, also arrived. Kitchener had five gun boats and 2,000 men; Marchand had seven officers and 120 troops. Faced with this impossible position Marchand withdrew.

In Britain and France the incident was seen as a symbol of the greater Anglo-French clash in Africa. Public opinion in both countries became inflamed and there was even talk of war. Neither government wanted to fight and war was avoided. The incident nevertheless showed that Anglo-French rivalry was as intense as ever.

Paul Kruger (1825–1904). Of German origin, he was president of the Transvaal Republic from 1883–1900; his two aims were to oppose British policy and spread the frontiers of the Transvaal; during the Boer war he travelled to Europe to try and find support and allies for the Boers; after the war he settled in Holland.

Horatio Herbert Kitchener (1850–1916). He spent much of his military career in Egypt, and in 1898 he conquered the Sudan; he commanded the British forces in the Boer War, and was commander-in-chief in India from 1902–9; he became earl Kitchener of Khartoum in 1914 and was made secretary of state for war when the First World war began; he was drowned in 1916 when the ship in which he was sailing to Russia hit a mine and sank.

South Africa

South Africa developed in a different way from the rest of the continent, for Europeans (mostly Dutch) settled there from the seventeenth century onwards. Britain seized the Cape in 1795, but relations with the Dutch settlers (the Boers) were always bad. When Britain tried to enforce racial equality before the law and to abolish slavery, many Dutch settlers pushed inland. This Great Trek from 1835 to 1838 led to the establishment of two Boer republics, Transvaal and the Orange Free State. Another Boer state, Natal, was founded in 1839 but was annexed by Britain in 1843. In the same year Britain announced her protectorship over Basutoland, which lay between Cape Colony and Natal. She annexed it in 1868. In 1876 Britain seized the Transvaal, but failed to hold it. At the convention of Pretoria in 1881 she recognised the independence of the Transvaal (or South African) Republic under president Paul Kruger.

Anglo-Boer Relations, 1881–99

Britain hoped to persuade the Boers to enter a federation of South African states under British rule. The plan was partly based on fears that the prosperity of the republics would surpass that of the colonies. The Suez canal, which shortened the route to India, threatened the importance of the Cape as the chief port between Europe and India. In the 1880s gold was discovered in the Transvaal and large numbers of prospectors poured in. It seemed that in future Transvaal would have a greater population and a stronger economy than the Cape.

The most aggressive supporter of the British cause was Cecil Rhodes, who was head of the South Africa Company and premier of the Cape from 1890 to 1896. His attempts to persuade Kruger to enter a federation failed. Rhodes therefore plotted to destroy the Transvaal, which he saw as a menace to the British in South Africa. He played on the grievances of the non-Dutch newcomers to the Transvaal (the 'Outlanders'), who paid extremely heavy taxes and were denied the vote. Rhodes hoped to persuade them to rebel, and offered military support which would be led from Bechuanaland by L. Starr Jameson.

The Outlanders, however, were unenthusiastic. Jameson grew impatient and decided that if he invaded, the Outlanders would rise and overthrow Kruger. In December 1895 he raided the Transvaal but the attack was a fiasco. There was no rebellion and Jameson and his followers were captured. A British parliamentary enquiry into the raid was set up. It found that Rhodes was clearly implicated and he resigned his premiership. The colonial secretary, Joseph Chamberlain, was found innocent of any knowledge of the plot. Later historical research indicates that in fact he was involved.

Anglo-Boer relations were now worse than ever. Kruger imported arms and passed a number of anti-alien laws. The British government became convinced that the only way to

Cecil John Rhodes (1853–1902). Financier, industrialist, supporter of British imperial rule; born in England he went to South Africa in 1874 and by 1889 was chairman of the De Beers Consolidated Mines Company; he became prime minister of the Cape in 1890 and hoped to subject most of Africa to Britain and build a railway from the Cape to Cairo; he was strongly opposed by Kruger and had to resign his premiership after the disgrace of the Jameson raid; during the Boer war he toured Britain and Europe seeking support for his cause, and he returned to Africa just before his death.

Boer fighters in action.

Joseph Chamberlain (1836–1914). British politician and one of the leading imperialist statesmen.

establish a federation was by war. In 1899 an Englishman in the Transvaal was shot by a policeman. The British Outlanders claimed that this was an act of tyranny and appealed to the British government, which supported their claims for equality with the Boers. Kruger rejected the British position, and in October 1899, supported by the Orange Free State, he sent an ultimatum demanding that Britain keep out of Transvaal affairs. The ultimatum was rejected and war broke out.

The Boer War and its Sequel

The war lasted until 1902, and although Britain won she did so with extreme difficulty. The British army was badly organised, slow-moving, and unfitted to cope with the open country and mobile Boers. Eventually 500,000 British troops were needed to defeat the farmer army. Britain's military prestige declined heavily as a result.

By 1902 the Transvaal and the Orange Free State were occupied, and their governments compelled to negotiate. Peace was signed at Vereeniging in that year, when the republics became crown colonies and Britain promised to restore their prosperity and recognise the Dutch language.

Reconstruction went ahead. The Transvaal in 1906 and the Orange Free State in 1907 received self-government. In 1908 plans were made for a customs union of the South African territories, but it was clear that political union was needed first. Later in 1908 a national convention met in Durban and drew up plans for such a union. It was established in 1910, and the first prime minister of the Union of South Africa was a Boer, Louis Botha.

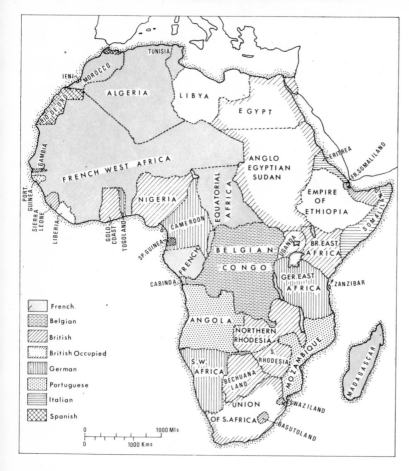

Africa in 1914.

The Anglo-French *Entente*

The Fashoda incident confirmed British supremacy along the Nile, while the Boer war confirmed it in South Africa. Meanwhile the French government had faced a number of internal crises and was anxious to avoid trouble overseas. The British, too, desired a settlement in Africa, and in 1904 reached an *entente* with France, just as they were to do with Russia in 1907. It was agreed that Britain's primacy in Egypt should not be hindered by France; in return Britain would allow France to dominate Algeria and Morocco. The long conflict between Britain and France finally came to an end.

Things to Do

1. Imagine yourself a foreign trader in China; give an account of your day-to-day affairs.
2. Find out more about the Boxer rising. How would you justify the Boxer cause, and how would you argue against it?

144

3. Find out more about early missionary work in Africa. To what extent did missionaries take European civilisation to Africa as well as Christianity?
4. Read about the Boers in the nineteenth century, and examine in particular the ways in which they tackled the problem of settlement.

Books to Read or Consult

K. S. Latourette, *A History of Modern China*, London 1954.

J. Marlowe, *Anglo-Egyptian Relations, 1800-1953*, London 1954.

R. Robinson and J. Gallagher, *Africa and the Victorians. The Official Mind of Imperialism*, London 1967.

French cartoon showing Morocco being pursued by Germany, France, England and Spain.

The First World War: Its Origins and Course

Emperor Francis Joseph I (1830–1916).

The Nationalities Problem in Austria

After the Franco-Prussian war the main centre of unrest moved from western to central and eastern Europe, and in particular to the Austrian empire. It was a multi-national empire based mainly on loyalty to the Habsburg dynasty. After 1848, however, the spread of nationalism meant that the subjects of the empire increasingly gave their loyalty to their 'nation' rather than to the Habsburgs. National groups demanded special concessions (which will be discussed later) which, added to Austria's defeats in Italy and Germany, indicated that the empire was rapidly declining.

The National Groups

According to the 1910 census the empire contained three main national groups. Out of a total population of about 51,500,000 the Germans made up 24%, the Magyars about 20% and the Slavs just over 47%. It is obvious from the figures that many of the empire's subjects were Slavs, but they did not form a single nation. They were made up of the following groups:

	% of population of empire
Czechs	13%
Poles	10%
Ruthenes	8%
Croats	5%
Serbs	4%
Slovaks	4%
Slovenes	3%

The Magyars

In the 1850s and 1860s the Habsburgs had most trouble with the Magyars in Hungary. A proud people with a strong sense of nationalism, they demanded virtual self-government from the emperor Francis Joseph I. After many years of resistance, the Habsburg government was forced to agree. In 1867, the year after defeat by Prussia, a compromise (the *Ausgleich*) was reached with the Magyars. Hungary was to be self-governing, but would recognise Francis Joseph as king of Hungary. Austria and Hungary were to have the same ministers for foreign affairs,

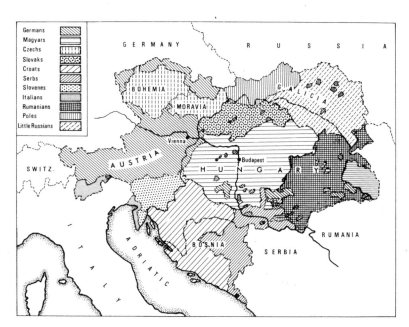

Nationalities in the Habsburg
Empire about 1900.

finance and the army. Their two parliaments were to appoint
delegations who would meet to vote on matters of common
interest. Henceforth the empire was known as Austria-Hungary.

The Czechs

The Czechs, who also wanted concessions from the Habsburgs, resented the *Ausgleich*, for it had been reached without
consulting them or any other national group. They hoped
eventually to see the empire as a federation of equal states.
This pressure was resisted by the Habsburgs who wanted direct
control over as much of the empire as possible, and by the
Magyars who, now that they had what they wanted, were prepared to support the emperor.

The Germans

Germans in the empire viewed the Slav movement with
concern. They despised the Slavs and feared that if they achieved
self-government, then Germans would suffer persecution in
Slav areas. In Hungary, Magyars were now oppressing non-
Magyars and Germans feared that similar developments would
follow in Slav-dominated parts of the empire. The answer, many
Germans thought, was to keep the Slavs firmly under the control
of Vienna and to refuse concessions to them. Many Germans
also suspected, however, that the emperor could not be trusted
to do this. Already in 1867 he had given in to the Magyars, and
he might also surrender to the Slavs.

This fear was strong among Germans in Bohemia, for they

made up only about 37% of the population there, most of the rest being Czechs. There grew up in Bohemia a powerful German nationalism as well as Czech nationalism. Extremists such as George von Schönerer appeared who organised German rallies, marches and demonstrations against the Czechs, and who demanded a united empire based on German supremacy.

The German nationalist movement in Bohemia also tended towards separatism. Many of those who doubted the ability of the Habsburgs to resist Slav pressure preferred to leave the empire and be joined to Germany rather than live in a Slav-dominated state. Politically this view expressed itself in the German National Union party, formed in 1887. By no means all Germans shared this outlook, but it found much support in Bohemia.

German fears were heightened in 1897 when the Austrian prime minister conceded to the Czechs that Bohemia would be administered through Czech and German instead of only German. This meant that civil servants would have to be bilingual, but whereas all educated Czechs spoke German, few Germans spoke Czech, and so the Czechs would take over the civil service of Bohemia. All over the empire Germans protested and in Bohemia itself there was widespread rioting. The decree was withdrawn but German suspicion of the emperor remained.

Suspicion was heightened in 1907 when the empire adopted universal suffrage. Since the Slavs outnumbered the Germans this meant that political influence had swung in their favour. It seemed to many Germans that drastic measures were needed to stop the advance of the Slavs.

The Balkan States

Another empire facing the problem of nationalism was Turkey. Nationalism was very strong in the Balkans where the Slavs were seeking independence. To make matters worse for Turkey, Austria-Hungary and Russia each wanted to replace her as the chief power in the Balkans. They had similar, although not identical, motives. They were faced with serious internal problems which they wished to offset by successes in foreign policy. Neither wanted to annex Balkan territory as this would rouse great opposition among the other powers. Instead they wished to turn the Balkans into a sphere of influence so that effective control could be gained without all the problems of international treaties.

Russia was helped by the fact that many Balkan Slavs looked to her as their natural protector. They hoped that she would head a movement to liberate Slavs from foreign rule and establish a united Slav state in eastern Europe.

The Break-up of the Balkans

Turkish authority in the Balkans steadily declined. Serbia became independent in 1829 and Greece in 1830. In 1875 Turkey's remaining Balkan territories rebelled. Russia intervened, swept across the Balkans and forced Turkey to accept her terms at the treaty of San Stefano in March 1878. Serbian independence was confirmed, and Montenegro and Rumania were also to be independent. Bosnia-Herzegovina was to be self-governing under Turkish sovereignty, while Bulgaria was to be independent and occupied by the Russians.

These terms led to an international outcry, for they amounted to Turkey's replacement by Russia as the leading Balkan power. So severe was the opposition of the other great powers that Russia agreed to attend an international conference in Berlin later in 1878 to revise the treaty of San Stefano. At Berlin it was agreed that Bulgaria should be divided into three parts: a smaller, independent Bulgaria; East Rumelia, to be administered by Turkey, but under a Christian governor; Macedonia, which would remain inside the Turkish empire. Bosnia-Herzegovina was to be administered by Austria-Hungary, although Turkey retained sovereignty. The independence of Serbia, Rumania and Montenegro was confirmed. The Congress of Berlin thus stemmed Russian ascendancy in the Balkans and brought Austria-Hungary in to balance Russia there.

The Balkans after 1878

After 1878 Austro-Hungarian diplomacy gradually diminished the influence of Russia and turned most of the Balkans into a sphere of Habsburg influence. In 1881 Serbia allied with Austria-Hungary, and in 1883 so did Rumania. Three years later the pro-Russian king of Bulgaria was deposed and replaced by a pro-Austrian. Habsburg supremacy over Russia in the Balkans did not receive a setback until 1903 when the unpopular king Alexander I of Serbia was murdered by army officers who set up a new dynasty under Peter I. During his reign Serbian policy became strongly anti-Habsburg and pro-Russian.

The Crisis of 1908

Serbia became the greatest headache to Austria-Hungary, for she encouraged the Slav movement there by urging the Slavs to make more and more demands on the Habsburgs. It was also widely believed that the Serbian prime minister, Pašić, dreamed of repeating the unification of Italy in the Balkans. He saw himself as the Balkan Cavour, with Serbia imitating the role of Piedmont-Sardinia. If such a project came to pass then Austro-

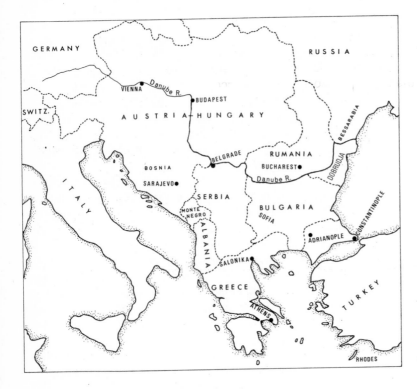

The Balkan States in 1914.

Hungarian influence in the Balkans would come to an end and she would suffer another defeat as she had in Italy.

The Habsburg government therefore wanted to thwart Pašić's schemes. Aehrenthal, foreign minister of Austria-Hungary, believed that he had the solution. Austria-Hungary must make a bold stroke in foreign policy by annexing Bosnia-Herzogovina, where Serbian influence was extremely powerful. Such a measure would solve several difficulties. It would demonstrate Austria-Hungary's determination to remain supreme in the Balkans; it would damage Pašić's prestige; it would discourage those Slavs in the Habsburg empire who looked to Serbia for leadership; it would prove to Germans in the empire that the Habsburgs were not giving in to Slav demands.

In 1908 Austria-Hungary thus annexed Bosnia-Herzogovina. Serbia was outraged but helpless unless Russia was prepared to give support. Russia, however, had recently suffered defeat by Japan and had been through a revolution. When Germany, who had allied with Austria-Hungary in 1879, announced her recognition of the annexation and sent an ultimatum to Russia that she too must accept it, Russia dared not stand by Serbia. The annexation went through and Austria-Hungary's position in the Balkans was confirmed.

150

The 'league of the three emperors'. Francis Joseph I of Austria-Hungary, William I of Germany and Alexander II of Russia, Berlin 1872.

The Wars of 1912–13

Although relations between the Balkan states were far from friendly, in 1912 Serbia, Bulgaria, Greece and Montenegro formed the Balkan League to expel Turkey finally from the Balkans. In October 1912 they declared war on Turkey and had defeated her by early 1913. Peace was signed at London in May 1913. The victors received Turkey's Balkan possessions, and the new state of Albania was set up at Austria-Hungary's insistence. Serbia wanted that region as an outlet to the sea, but Austria-Hungary, as part of her policies against Serbia, secured its establishment as an independent state.

Trouble in the Balkans was not yet over. Bulgaria suspected Greece and Serbia of wanting to take most of the spoils of the recent war, and so declared war on them. She was beaten within a few weeks, but not before Greece and Serbia had been joined by Turkey, who wanted to recapture some of her lost territories, and Rumania, who wanted the Bulgarian region of Dobrudja to give her an outlet to the sea. Peace was eventually signed at Bucharest in August 1913, when Serbia and Greece received Bulgaria's share of the ex-Turkish provinces, Turkey acquired Adrianople, and Rumania duly received Dobrudja.

Other International Developments

In western Europe, where Germany had replaced France as the leading power, the period from 1871 to 1890 was dominated by Bismarck's measures to keep France diplomatically isolated. He knew that France would try to restore her supremacy, but could only make a move if she had strong allies.

Bismarck began this policy shortly after the Franco-Prussian war. In 1872 he secured a meeting of the emperors of Austria-Hungary, Germany and Russia in Berlin, and they agreed upon

Punch cartoon on the dismissal of Bismarck by kaiser William II in 1890.

DROPPING THE PILOT

151

an *entente*. The 'league of the three emperors' collapsed when Russia and Austria-Hungary fell out over the Balkans in the 1870s, but Bismarck signed an alliance with Austria-Hungary in 1879 (the Dual Alliance). Two years later he signed a treaty with Russia (renewed in 1884 and 1887) by which Russia agreed to stay neutral in any future Franco-German war. In 1882 Italy joined the Dual Alliance. No treaty was signed with Britain, but it was pointed out in the last chapter that Bismarck encouraged disagreement between France and Britain in Africa, and so ensured against their signing an alliance.

In 1890 Bismarck was dismissed by the young kaiser William II, under whom German policy gradually abandoned Bismarck's principles. Later that year the German government refused to renew the treaty with Russia, who in 1893 allied with France. This was exactly what Bismarck had wanted to avoid. French isolation ended, and her agreement with Russia stated that if Germany attacked either of them, then the other would fight Germany.

Britain and Germany

At the turn of the century relations between Britain and Germany began to decline. Germany gave open support to the Boers, and in 1900 the second German Naval Act made provision to build a large number of battleships so that Germany could rival Britain in the North Sea. There was a strong reaction from the British, who themselves began the rapid construction of more warships. Thus, while on the one hand Britain established good relations with her ex-rivals France and Russia through the *ententes* of 1904 and 1907, her relations with Germany became strained.

Kaiser William II.

German Foreign Policy after 1900

During the first decade of this century German foreign policy became aggressive as she sought to confirm her supremacy in western Europe by humiliating France. In 1905 William II visited Morocco and there announced that she should be free of French influence. A conference of powers at Algeciras in 1906, however, confirmed France's position in Morocco (only Austria-Hungary stood by Germany), and so Germany rather than France received a setback.

William tried again in 1911. French troops occupied the town of Fez to help the sultan of Morocco to suppress a rebellion. William denounced this 'invasion' and sent a gunboat to the Moroccan port of Agadir. Britain as well as France was disturbed at this move, for here was an example of German naval strength supporting diplomacy. Britain threatened to go to war

The archduke Francis Ferdinand and his wife start out on the drive during which they were assassinated on 28 June 1914, Sarajevo.

unless Germany stopped her bullying tactics. William backed down and acknowledged French control of Morocco.

By 1914, therefore, Germany had poor relations with France, Russia (whom she had humiliated by the ultimatum of 1908) and Britain.

Sarajevo, 1914

In the Balkans, Austria-Hungary was in a strong position. The nationalities problem had lessened, Serbia was weak after her wars, and Russia still had not rebuilt her forces after the defeat by Japan. In June 1914 Austria-Hungary held army manoeuvres in Bosnia. The heir to the Habsburg throne, the archduke Francis Ferdinand, went with his wife to inspect the manoeuvres, and on 28 June visited the Bosnian capital, Sarajevo. They were assassinated by a young Serb, Gavrilo Princip.

In the outcry that followed, the Habsburg government saw a chance to accuse the Serbian government of having been involved in the murder, to humiliate it and deal another heavy blow to Serbian prestige. First, however, it was necessary to know the attitude of Germany.

William II informed the Austrians that they had Germany's full support. If Russia stood by Serbia they were not to be deterred, for Germany was prepared to fight Russia if necessary. Having committed Germany to support whatever Austria-Hungary did, William went off on a cruise.

Assured of German backing, Austria-Hungary sent an ultimatum to Serbia on 23 July that included a demand that Austrian officials should enter Serbia to root out anti-Austrian elements. Serbia accepted the ultimatum except for the statement

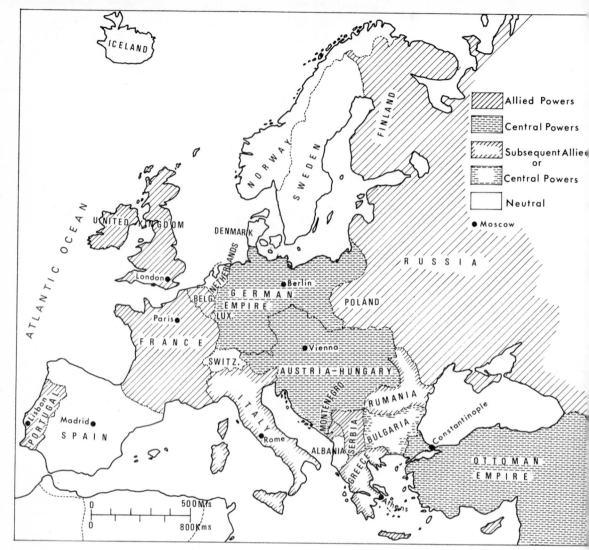

Europe in 1914.

on Austrian officials. This did not satisfy Austria-Hungary, who declared war on 28 July.

The Position of Russia

On 24 July Serbia had appealed for help to Russia, who began to mobilise in an attempt to warn Austria-Hungary to treat Serbia lightly. Russian generals warned their government that partial mobilisation was pointless, for behind Austria-Hungary was Germany, who would rather fight than back down; thus Russia either must mobilise fully and be prepared for war, or do nothing and leave Serbia to her fate, which would mean humiliation for Russia. The tsar himself stepped in and ordered full mobilisation.

ARMÉE DE TERRE ET ARMÉE DE MER

ORDRE
DE MOBILISATION GÉNÉRALE

Par décret du Président de la République, la mobilisation des armées de terre et de mer est ordonnée, ainsi que la réquisition des animaux, voitures et harnais nécessaires au complément de ces armées.

Le premier jour de la mobilisation est le Dimanche 2 Août 1914

Tout Français soumis aux obligations militaires doit, sous peine d'être puni avec toute la rigueur des lois, obéir aux prescriptions du **FASCICULE DE MOBILISATION** (pages coloriées placées dans son livret).

Sont visés par le présent ordre **TOUS LES HOMMES** non présents sous les Drapeaux et appartenant :

1° à l'**ARMÉE DE TERRE** y compris les **TROUPES COLONIALES** et les hommes des **SERVICES AUXILIAIRES;**

2° à l'**ARMÉE DE MER** y compris les **INSCRITS MARITIMES** et les **ARMURIERS** de la **MARINE.**

Les Autorités civiles et militaires sont responsables de l'exécution du présent décret.

Le Ministre de la Guerre.   *Le Ministre de la Marine.*

The warning of the generals proved correct, for Germany declared war on Russia on 1 August; Austria-Hungary did so on 5 August.

Germany, France and Britain

The German government was in fact in a difficult position, for the army had only one plan of war, the Schlieffen plan. It had been drawn up by count Alfred von Schlieffen, German chief of staff from 1891 to 1905. He believed that if Germany went to war it would be against Russia and France. This meant that Germany must fight on two fronts, and his plan was intended to deal with this possibility. It gambled on slow Russian mobilisation, and provided for a rapid attack on France through Belgium; Paris would fall in forty days, France would make peace, and the whole German army could then go east to fight the Russians.

The trouble was that on 1 August Germany was at war with

155

French soldiers on their way to war.

Russia but not with France, whereas the Schlieffen plan said that France must be fought first. Thus Germany must bring France into the war before Russian mobilisation advanced too far. The German government therefore provoked a crisis with France and on 3 August declared war on her.

Much opinion in Britain supported France against Germany, but the government hoped to stay neutral. On 2 August it announced that Britain would remain neutral if the German fleet kept out of the English Channel, and if the neutrality of

James Keir Hardie (1856–1915). First independent Labour Member of Parliament in Britain; he was brought up in Scotland where he worked in mines by day and studied at night; he was an energetic union worker, and helped to form the Scottish Labour Party in 1889 and the Independent Labour Party in 1893; he was an M.P. from 1892–5 and from 1900–15; a staunch pacifist he wanted socialists all over Europe to take no part in the First World war.

156

British soldiers face out across 'no man's land' or the area between trenches of the opposing armies.

Belgium was respected. The Schlieffen plan, however, included the invasion of Belgium, which the Germans began on 3 August when they declared war on France. The following day Britain declared war on Germany.

The Spread of the War

Within the few days between 28 July and 4 August 1914 the European powers found themselves at war. Later in the year Turkey joined the central powers (Germany and Austria-Hungary), but Japan declared war on Germany and attacked her possessions in the Far East. The war spread further in 1915 when Italy joined the *entente* powers and Bulgaria joined the central powers. In 1916 Rumania, and in 1917 the U.S.A., joined the *entente* powers.

The Failure of the Schlieffen plan

Unfortunately for the Germans the Schlieffen plan failed. Russia mobilised more quickly than was expected and in mid-August invaded Germany. The Belgians put up stiffer resistance than was foreseen, for Liège held out for twelve days. The French, aided by the British, defended their northern frontier and blocked the line of German advance. The Germans tried a change of plan and attacked down the river Marne in September. Once more they were foiled as reinforcements were rushed to defend the Marne. The failure of the attack led to a German retreat. Both sides set up a defensive line of trenches which eventually stretched from the sea to the Swiss border.

Barbed wire formed a barrier
against infantry attacks.

Heavy guns pounded the infantry
lined up in the trenches.

The British tank, a new weapon introduced in 1916.

German soldiers wearing gas masks during a gas attack. The soldier in the centre has just released a dog carrying a message.

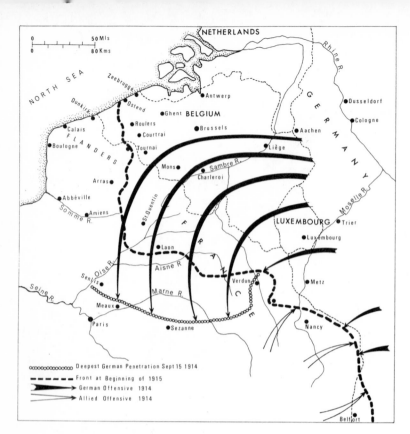

The First World war: the Western Front.

A fighter plane of the 1914–18 war.

The War on the Western Front

The war in the west was a slogging match between two heavyweights who lacked speed and finesse. The general pattern soon established itself. Complex barbed wire entanglements were laid in front of trenches where there were troops armed with repeating rifles and machine guns. They formed an almost invincible barrier against mass infantry attacks.

Both sides tried to overcome the supremacy of defence over attack by searching for new weapons. In 1915 the Germans first used chlorine gas, which, although deadly, had to be carried to the enemy by the wind, which could change and blow the gas back on the Germans.

The principal new British weapon was the tank, introduced in 1916. It was hoped that the tank would be able to barge its way through barbed wire, and protect its crew from bullets by its armour plating. The early tanks, however, were too cumbersome to be effective. Their maximum speed was only three to four miles per hour, and over rough ground they barely reached one mile per hour. In the mud along the western front they simply stuck. Improvements were made, and in the later stages of the war the tanks played a significant role.

Machine guns were used with dreadful effect during mass infantry attacks.

A scene of battlefield desolation during the war, an area where nothing lives.

160

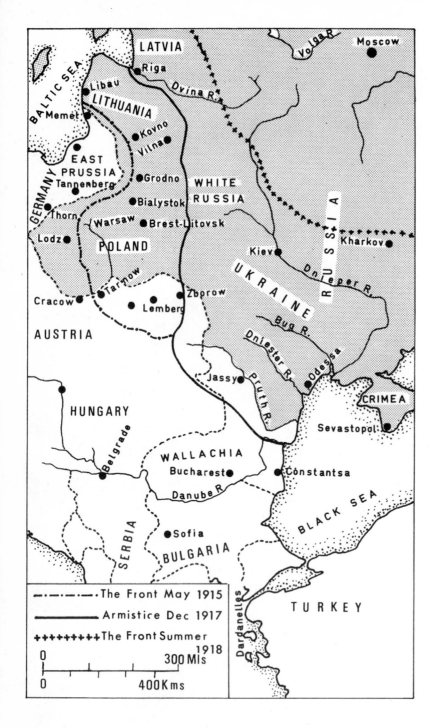

The First World war: the Eastern
Front.

The Gallipoli Campaign. The campaign lasted from February 1915 to January 1916 and was an attempt, mainly by the British, to open a sea link between the Black Sea and the Mediterranean by seizing the Turkish peninsula commanding the route; the campaign was a failure and resulted in heavy casualties.

The kaiser consults his commanders, field-marshal Hindenburg (left) and general Ludendorff (right).

British and French leaders. From left: general Joffre, president Poincaré, king George V, general Foch and Sir Douglas Haig.

163

A German U-boat brings news to a small submarine, 1917.

The other military development was the aeroplane. At first it was used only for spotting purposes, but by the end of the war it was equipped with machine guns, and also carried out bombing raids along the trench lines.

In spite of the superiority of defensive measures over attack, commanders on both sides, but especially the French, had a blind faith in the mass infantry charge. It was usually launched on the enemy's strong points, the theory being that if a break-through came there, then his whole defensive line would fall back in confusion. The futility of this theory is seen in the fact that between 1914 and 1918 the trench line never moved more than a few miles in any direction. The war on the western front was fought on a comparatively narrow strip of land between the North Sea and Switzerland.

This insistence on infantry attacks against well defended positions helps to explain the heavy casualty rates. In 1915 the British offensive at Neuve Chapelle between 10 and 13 March cost 13,000 casualties. At the battle of Vimy Ridge in 1915 the French suffered almost 100,000 casualties and the Germans 75,000. The battle of the Somme, which lasted for several months in 1916, resulted in over 400,000 British, 195,000 French, and 650,000 German dead and wounded.

The War on the Eastern Front

In eastern Europe the Russian attack on Germany was halted in 1914 by German victories at Tannenberg and at the Masurian Lakes. Thereafter stalemate set in. Russia's armies were too ill-equipped and poorly led to break through. The armies of Austria-Hungary were inefficient and failed to defeat Serbia. Furthermore, when Italy entered the war in 1915 Austria-Hungary had to divert troops to fight the Italians. Germany had

164

A captured German U-boat, 1917.

too many troops on the western front to conduct effective campaigns in the east, and although in 1915 the Germans pushed back the Russians two hundred miles, there was no question of Germany alone defeating Russia.

The war on the eastern front was greatly influenced by events inside Russia. In 1917 the tsarist regime was overthrown, the country fell into chaos, Russia's armies disintegrated, the Bolsheviks seized power and sought peace, which was signed with Germany at Brest-Litovsk in 1918. This is discussed in more detail later, but the immediate effect was to release more German soldiers for the western front.

The War at Sea

During the war it was expected that the British and German fleets would meet to decide who ruled the seas. The clash came in 1916 when the German High Seas Fleet sailed out to try and trap the British Grand Fleet. They met at the battle of Jutland, but there was no full scale conflict as the British outmanoeuvred the Germans and forced them to retreat back to port, where they remained bottled up for the rest of the war. Even so, the German fleet inflicted considerable damage on the British at Jutland, for the Grand Fleet lost fourteen ships (including three battleships) as against eleven ships on the German side.

The German naval threat to Britain came principally from submarines (U-boats) which inflicted heavy losses on her. In

American troops arrive in Europe.

1917 over 4,000,000 tons of British merchant shipping were sunk, and losses on this scale threatened to destroy Britain's trade and force her out of the war. The answer was found by prime minister Lloyd George, who insisted on sending ships in convoys protected by warships. The first sailed in February 1917. The system was a success, which was shown in 1918 when under 2,000,000 tons of shipping were destroyed.

The Entry of the U.S.A. into the War

In 1915 Germany announced that neutral ships within a certain area around the British and Irish coasts were liable to be attacked by U-boats. This offended the American government, and a huge public outcry occurred in the U.S.A. when a U-boat sank a passenger ship, the 'Lusitania', just off the Irish coast in May 1915. Over 1,000 people lost their lives, including 128 Americans. The American government protested so strongly that there was even talk of war. The Germans therefore promised not to sink passenger ships without warning.

In January 1917, however, Germany announced unrestricted submarine warfare, and within the next few weeks sank several American ships. Throughout the entire U.S.A. Germany was now seen as an enemy, and on 6 April 1917 the American government declared war on her. The U.S.A. refused, however, to sign an alliance with Britain, France and Russia; she entered the war as an 'associated' power.

The End of the War

By the end of 1917 both sides wanted peace. In Germany this desire grew even stronger in 1918, for as American involvement in the war increased, and outstripped the advantage to

Germany of Russia's withdrawal, military defeat faced the Germans. In July 1918 they attempted a last grand offensive on the western front, but it was halted and Germany's enemies began to advance.

Inside Germany there was deep unrest and even the threat of revolution. Her allies, Turkey, Bulgaria and Austria-Hungary, were either defeated or facing collapse, and the German government decided that the war must be stopped as soon as possible. On 11 November 1918 an armistice was signed and the First World war came to an end.

Peace Negotiations

In January 1918 the American president, Woodrow Wilson, gave a speech to Congress on 'Fourteen Points for World Peace'. He put forward three great principles: national self-government should be established everywhere; diplomacy and international agreements should be made public; a League of Nations should be set up, in which international problems could be discussed and through which small states could be protected against the aggression of larger ones.

After the armistice a conference of twenty-seven nations met at Paris to draw up a peace treaty. Germany was not represented until most of the agreements had been reached, and the final terms were simply presented to her for acceptance. The negotiations were dominated by Britain, France, Italy and the U.S.A. (Russia was not present as she had withdrawn from the war in 1918), and peace was signed at Versailles on 28 June 1919.

The treaty makers, from left: Orlando of Italy, Lloyd George of Great Britain, Clemenceau of France and Wilson of the U.S.A.

A French child, at her father's grave, asks 'Does daddy know that we have won?'.

The Peace Terms

In the settlement, all Germany's colonies were surrendered, and in Europe she handed over Alsace-Lorraine to France, northern Schleswig to Denmark, Eupen-Malmédy to Belgium, and part of west Prussia and Upper Silesia to Poland. The industrially important Saar basin was to be occupied by the allies for fifteen years and then kept free of all armed forces. Germany's army was to be limited to 100,000 men and was to have no tanks or heavy artillery; her navy was to have only six battleships and a few smaller ships; she was to have no submarines or airforce; most of her merchant ships were to be given up. Two further clauses created much opposition in Germany to the terms. One was the War Guilt clause which laid all responsibility for the war with Germany. The other said that Germany was to pay reparations to her war-time enemies for the damage she had caused.

Many Germans regarded the territorial losses in the peace, and the occupation of the Saar by the French, as harsh. The War Guilt clause was resented, for while many people did not deny that Germany was partly responsible for the war, they did not agree that she was wholly to blame. The amount of reparations to be paid was not fixed until 1921, when it was announced that Germany must pay over £6,000 million, and complaints soon spread that this was too much. Finally, when the League of Nations was set up Germany was refused membership; this too was greatly resented.

As far as Austria-Hungary was concerned, the settlement of 1919 recognised what was already a fact; the Habsburg empire had collapsed and out of its ruins independent states appeared. Czechoslovakia and Yugoslavia were formed, while Hungary

German signature to the treaty of Versailles.

28. Juni 1919

Europe after the First World war.

became fully independent. A smaller Austria was left as an independent republic.

There still remained the question of Poland and the Baltic states which had been seized from Russia by Germany in 1918. By now the government of Russia was in the hands of the Communists, whom the west European states regarded with intense distrust. In the nineteenth century Russia had often been seen as a threat to Europe, and so in 1919 the peacemakers decided to keep her out of Europe. Instead of returning the lost provinces to Russia, the peace terms set them up as the independent states of Finland, Estonia, Lithuania, Latvia and Poland.

The First World war completed the disintegration of the old empires and also marked the end of Europe's domination of the world. America's involvement in the war indicated that she was going to take a larger part in world affairs in future; the establishment of Communist Russia set up a political order totally different from that of the past; the League of Nations was intended to make old-fashioned European diplomacy unnecessary and to prevent expansionism by European states. President Wilson claimed that the peace had made the world safe for democracy; in effect he meant that European primacy was overthrown.

Things to Do

1. Read some of the contemporary accounts of the war: a good example is Robert Graves, *Goodbye to all that* (Penguin paperback).
2. Take one aspect of the military side of the war (e.g. the war at sea or the war in the air) and study its development.
3. Make a list of the war aims of the main powers; how far were these aims achieved?
4. What do you consider were the strong and weak points of the peace of 1919?

Books to Read or Consult

D. F. Fleming, *The Origins and Legacies of World War One*, London 1968.

M. Gilbert, *The European Powers, 1900-45*, London 1965.

A. J. P. Taylor, *The Habsburg Monarchy, 1809-1918*, London 1964.

A. J. P. Taylor, *The First World War: an Illustrated History*, London 1966.

L. C. F. Turner, *The First World War*, London 1967 (Warne's Modern History Monographs).

The Russian Revolution

Introduction

The First World war destroyed the east European empires of
Russia, Turkey and Austria-Hungary. In Russia there was revolution in 1917 which led to the creation of the first socialist state
in the history of the world.

Russia in 1917

Russia had long been considered the most backward state
in Europe, with the exception of the Turkish empire. Over
eighty per cent of the population were peasants; most of them
were illiterate, their agricultural methods were out of date, they
were among the poorest people in Europe, and they saw little
hope of improvement. They lived in a condition of permanent
discontent and posed the largest single social problem to the
government. There were few towns, and although industry was
spreading Russia was still industrially weak. The government
was inept. After the revolution of 1905 a parliament (*Duma*)
had been created, but the tsar retained much personal authority,
so that the country effectively remained under the rule of one
man. Russia, however, was too vast and the problems too many
for an autocrat to rule efficiently; moreover the tsar Nicholas II
lacked the strength of character to impose strong government.

During the First World war conditions declined drastically.
Industrial production fell, so did agricultural production, there
were food shortages, prices rose, the army suffered heavy
defeats, but the tsarist regime had no answers to these problems.

The February Revolution

On 8 March 1917 (23 February in the Russian calendar)
revolution broke out in the capital, Petrograd (the name was
changed from St. Petersburg in 1914) against the shortage of
food. This was no planned revolution, but a revolution of the
nineteenth-century type; it was spontaneous, for the masses simply rose to reject existing conditions, much as they had done
throughout Europe in 1848. The rioting spread, troops joined
in, and the *Duma* appealed to Nicholas II to form a new government. The tsar refused and tried to dismiss the *Duma*. It rejected
his orders and created a Provisional Government. On 15 March
Nicholas abdicated and the Provisional Government, headed
by Prince Lvov, took over. Nothing indicates the abysmal decline
of the monarchy so much as the ease with which the tsarist
regime collapsed under the pressure of a mass rising.

Revolution in Petrograd, 1917.

The Provisional Government

The Provisional Government was made up of moderates who hoped eventually to establish constitutional rule. There were, however, several immediate problems that had to be tackled, and with regard to these the government took unpopular decisions which dangerously undermined its support among the masses.

First there was the question of the war. Throughout Russia the desire for peace was swelling, but the government decided to fight on. It feared that Germany wanted to eliminate Russia as a European power; the government was also under strong pressure from Britain and France to continue fighting. This decision alienated large numbers of people.

In the provinces the peasants demanded wide agrarian reforms. Above all, they wanted the Provisional Government to hand over land to the peasants. The government refused to act, and announced that the peasants must wait until the war was finished before the land question could be tackled. The disgruntled peasants now began to turn against the Provisional Government.

The third factor that made the Provisional Government unpopular concerned nationalism. Within the Russian empire some nations, such as the Finns, the Estonians and the Ukranians, were demanding a certain amount of self-government. The government announced that like the peasants, the national groups must wait until the end of the war before their demands could be discussed. An exception was made of Poland, whose independence was recognised.

Grigori Efimovich Rasputin (1871–1916). The son of a Siberian peasant, he became the most influential person at the cou of tsar Nicholas II; the tsarina thought him a divinely sent figure who would save Russia; he was widely thought to have magical powers; he wielded considerable political power and was assassinated in 1916.

Lenin in 1918.

The Soviets

During the revolution, councils (soviets) had been formed by workers and troops to discuss the crisis and to formulate ideas for reform. The most important soviet was that of Petrograd, which held the allegiance of the city. Early in 1917 the soviets were the only bodies to command a great deal of public support. For the time being they recognised the authority of the Provisional Government, but, because of their mass support, had the ability to overthrow it if they wished.

The Russian Socialists

Most Russian socialists favoured direct revolution as the way to establish a socialist state, and therefore welcomed the events of March 1917. They were divided into bitterly quarrelling factions. One major group was the Socialist Revolutionaries, who used terrorism as a device to disrupt government. Another was the Marxist Social Democrats, who in 1903 had split between the Mensheviks and Bolsheviks. They followed the teaching of Karl Marx, but whereas the Mensheviks had tried to work through the *Duma* and had members within it, the Bolsheviks aimed at direct revolution.

The Mensheviks and Bolsheviks disagreed over the interpretation of the revolution in March. The Mensheviks said that it had put the middle classes into power (i.e. the Provisional Government), that Russia was not yet ready for socialism, and therefore that the Provisional Government should be supported. The Bolsheviks, led by Nicholai Lenin (1870–1924), agreed that the Provisional Government was middle class in character,

Alexander Feodorovich Kerensky (1881–1970). A lawyer who was elected to the Duma in 1912 as a socialist; in 1917 he became prime minister but failed to reorganise the army, win the support of the masses or suppress revolutionaries; when the Bolsheviks seized power he left the country and eventually went to live in the U.S.A.

173

but argued that it was so weak that it could be overthrown and Russia turned into a socialist state.

Lenin

Lenin, the son of a schoolmaster, was born at Simbirsk on the river Volga. He was baptised Vladimir Ilyich Ulyanov, but he assumed the name Lenin in 1901. His brother Alexander was executed in 1887 for being involved in a plot to kill tsar Alexander III. Lenin was horrified at his brother's death, and when he went that year to study law at Kazan University, he was a confirmed revolutionary. After a few months he was expelled for taking part in student demonstrations, but he continued his studies and received a degree from St. Petersburg University in 1891.

Meanwhile, he turned to the writings of Karl Marx and was converted by the power of their arguments. At this time the Russian revolutionary movement was broken into factions, none of which had clear plans for the future of Russia. Marxism, on the other hand, laid down guide lines to revolution which, Lenin believed, guaranteed success and would lead to the creation of a socialist state. When he went to live in St. Petersburg in 1893 he therefore went as an expert on Marxism, devoted to spreading Marxist theories.

His activities led him into trouble, and in 1897 he was exiled to Siberia for three years. After his release he spent most of the next seventeen years abroad, mainly in Switzerland. He ran a journal, *Iskra* (*The Spark*), which he sent into Russia and through which he attempted to keep Russian Marxists in line with his own thought. He always maintained a close interest in Russian Marxist affairs, and associated with the Bolsheviks in the split of 1903.

When the revolution broke out in 1917 Lenin was in Switzerland, and wanted to return to Russia to exploit the situation. The way back, however, was barred by the Germans. Nevertheless, they too were anxious to make the most of the turmoil in Russia, and allowed Lenin and other revolutionaries to travel to Russia in a special train; they calculated that Lenin would keep the disorders going and so weaken the Russian war effort.

When he arrived there Lenin, aided by Leon Trotsky (1877–1940), sought means whereby the Bolsheviks could seize power. He saw the answer in the soviets; since the soviets enjoyed mass support, if the Bolsheviks could control the soviets they would be well on the way to controlling Russia. Throughout 1917, therefore, the Bolsheviks infiltrated the soviets, especially the powerful Petrograd soviet. The campaign was a success, and by September 1917 the Petrograd soviet, and many others, had fallen under Bolshevik leadership.

Leon Davidovich Trotsky (1877–1940). His real name was Leib Davidovich Bronstein; a revolutionary who was exiled to Siberia, but in 1902 he joined Lenin in Britain; he became a Menshevik, but in 1917 returned to Russia to help the Bolsheviks; he played a leading role in the October Revolution and was made foreign minister in the Communist government; he created the Red army which defeated the Whites in the civil war, but was defeated in the struggle for leadership of the Communist Party after Lenin's death by Stalin; he was expelled from the Party in 1927 and exiled in 1929; he was assassinated by a Russian agent in Mexico in 1940.

The Decline of the Provisional Government

In contrast to the growing influence of the Bolsheviks, the authority of the Provisional Government was declining. In July 1917 there were spontaneous demonstrations in Petrograd demanding 'all power to the soviets'. Prince Lvov resigned as head of the Provisional Government, and was succeeded by Alexander Kerensky. The armies at the front were disintegrating under mass desertions. In September there was an attempted right wing coup, and by the end of the month the authority of the Provisional Government to all intents and purposes was gone.

The Bolshevik Revolution

Lenin and Trotsky believed that the time had come to seize power. They did so on the evening and the early morning of 6–7 November (25–26 October in the Russian calendar). Aided by sailors from the naval base at Kronstadt, the Bolsheviks took the Winter Palace in Petrograd where they arrested the members of the Provisional Government (except for Kerensky who was visiting the army). They set up a Council of Peoples' Commissars to govern the country; Lenin was chairman, Trotsky was put in charge of foreign affairs, and the rest of the council likewise were Bolsheviks.

Lenin addressed the All Russia Congress of Soviets and announced his plans. Elections were to be held for a Constituent Assembly, peace was to be signed with Germany, land would be taken over by special committees and distributed among the peasants, and all industrial affairs would be put under the control of the workers. At the same time the Bolsheviks changed their title to Communists.

The First Year of Communist Rule

Russia was falling into anarchy and Lenin knew that unless he moved carefully, Communist rule would be as short-lived as that of the Provisional Government. Indeed, some of his early decisions made his party unpopular. The first decision concerned the results of the elections for the Constituent Assembly. Of the votes cast, 62% went to the Socialist Revolutionaries, 13% went to various moderate parties, and only 25% to the Communists. When, therefore, the Constituent Assembly met in January 1918, it lasted only two days, for Lenin broke it up. This had been the first democratically elected political body in the history of Russia, and a good deal of anti-Communist feeling spread at Lenin's treatment of it. His explanation for having destroyed the Assembly was twofold. He claimed that the only representative bodies of the workers were the soviets, whereas the

Daughters of tsar Nicholas II, Olga (above) and Maria (below).

Constituent Assembly would be an instrument of the middle classes. He also maintained that the electors had not had time to appreciate the importance of the Bolshevik Revolution; if they had, they would have voted for the Communists; by breaking up the Assembly Lenin had saved them from their folly.

Another decision that damaged the prestige of the Communists was the peace terms accepted from Germany at Brest-Litovsk in March 1918. Russia surrendered to Germany a vast region including Poland and the Baltic Provinces, and granted independence to Finland and the Ukraine. These terms were the most humiliating that Russia had ever suffered.

In spite of their early unpopularity the Communists survived. Historians take different views on why they did so, but an explanation that many accept is that they were saved by the civil war which began in 1919 and lasted until 1922.

The Effect of the Civil War

The Russian civil war is a terrible story of anarchy, brutality and starvation. The two chief centres of opposition to the Communists were the steppes of Kuban and Siberia. In Siberia a rival government under admiral Kolchak set itself up, aided by the Japanese who had invaded the country. There was fighting also in the Ukraine, in the Baltic provinces and in the extreme north, where the British and French landed at the ports of Murmansk and Archangel.

The 'Whites' (as the anti-Communists were called) wanted

Olga, the eldest daughter of the tsar, surrounded by Bolshevik soldiers while in captivity.

176

Starving people wait patiently for bread during the 1921 famine in Russia.

to restore the landed estates to the aristocracy, destroy the Communists, and reimpose the pre-war social and political order. It was this that pushed many people in the towns and the countryside on to the side of the Communists in the civil war; it was also this that cast Lenin as the saviour of revolution and the champion of the people against the forces of reaction. Gradually the Whites were overcome and the foreigners expelled from the country. The Communists emerged victorious from the war, with their authority firmly established under Lenin.

The New Economic Policy

The economic life of the country had been ruined by the First World war and the civil war. Lenin turned to the question of reconstruction and in 1921 announced his New Economic Policy (N.E.P.). The N.E.P. provided for a mixture of socialism and private enterprise. Many Communists felt that Lenin should have introduced absolute socialism immediately, but he argued that the widespread ruin made it impossible. The N.E.P. aimed at nationalising and developing industry, and at restoring internal and external commerce.

Nationalisation of industry went ahead at a leisurely pace, and as late as 1927 almost 40% of Russian industrial enterprises were privately owned. Commercial contacts were made with

most other European states, the majority of which had recognised the Communist regime by 1924. So far as agriculture
was concerned, peasants were allowed to own land and sell
their produce at a profit.

It was the peasants, however, who threatened the success
of the N.E.P. Although they quickly restored agricultural production to its pre-war level, they sent less into the towns and
so created food shortages, rising food prices, and grumbling
among the workers. Lenin therefore sought means to persuade
the peasants to put a higher percentage of their crops on to the
urban markets. He did this in two ways. He made sure that they
were paid good prices for their products. He also imported,
and allowed some Russian industry to produce, consumer goods
which the peasants needed; the peasants were thus encouraged
to seek higher profits with which to buy the goods by sending
more food into the town markets.

The Political System

In theory the political basis of the new Russian state was the
soviets, as was shown by the title of the country, 'the Union of
Soviet Socialist Republics'. In practice the soviets were controlled by two central bodies, the Central Executive Committee
of the Congress of Soviets, and the Committee of Peoples'
Commissars. The Communist Party monopolised positions on
these committees and also extended its domination of the soviets,
from which it expelled Mensheviks and Socialist Revolutionaries. In other words, by the early 1920s it was not so much
the power of the soviets which distinguished the political life
of the state, as the power of the Communist Party.

The Communist Party

The chief body of the Communist Party was the Central
Committee, which was elected by the Party Congress. In 1919

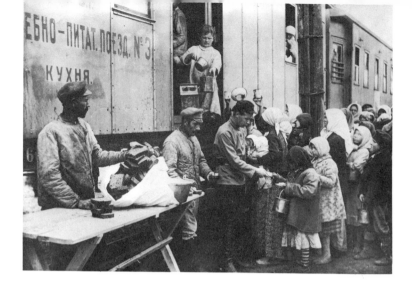

Food being handed out to hungry crowds from a relief train, Russia 1921.

two other bodies were created to serve the Central Committee; the Politbureau, which was concerned with political affairs, and the Orgbureau, which organised the party. In the 1920s the Politbureau gradually took over many of the powers of the Central Committee and became the most influential authority in the state. In 1922 the post of Secretary General was established, and given to Joseph Stalin (1879–1953) who was already a member of the Politbureau and Orgbureau.

By 1923 Stalin was one of the most powerful individuals in the Communist Party, for as well as his three positions just mentioned, he headed the Rabkrin, whose function was to keep the civil service under the control of the party. When Lenin fell seriously ill in 1923 and the question of his successor became imminent, Stalin's name was considered.

The Struggle for Power

Lenin died on 21 January 1924. Of the contenders for leadership of the party the figure with most prestige was Trotsky, who had masterminded the Bolshevik revolution. His opponent Stalin, supported by Zinoviev and Kamenev, accused him of being an opportunist who had not joined the Bolsheviks until 1917, prior to which he had been a Menshevik. Trotsky retorted that Stalin, Zinoviev and Kamenev had been hesitant over the revolution in 1917, and only gave it their full support when success had been won. Trotsky also accused Stalin of having allowed the civil service to assume too much authority. It was a mistake on Trotsky's part to attack these three powerful men and the civil service at the same time. He was dismissed as head of the armed forces in January 1925, and thereafter his position declined until he was dismissed from the party in 1927.

A quarrel then broke out in 1925 between Stalin on one side and Zinoviev and Kamenev (aided by the weakened Trotsky) on

Joseph Stalin (1879–1953).

the other. Zinoviev, Kamenev and Trotsky maintained that because the industrialisation programme was moving slowly owing to the peasant problem, the answer was to impose heavier taxes on the peasants and invest the money thus raised in industry. Stalin replied that such a policy would be simply a form of exploitation of the peasants, more typical of the tsarist regime than of the Communists. Stalin won a great deal of support among the peasants for this stand.

On another question, Zinoviev, Kamenev and Trotsky urged that the U.S.S.R. should encourage socialist revolutions elsewhere in Europe; new socialist states would then give help to socialist Russia. Stalin disagreed, proclaiming that Russia could create a socialist state alone. Stalin once more won popularity by his argument, for most Russians were unwilling to risk a new war for the sake of revolutions abroad.

The Party Congress of December 1925 gave Stalin its backing on these questions, and so put him ahead in the struggle for leadership. In 1927 it confirmed his lead when it not only expelled Trotsky from the party, but Zinoviev and Kamenev too.

Stalin's triumph was almost complete. He had powerful critics in Bukharin, editor of *Pravda* (the party newspaper), and Tomsky, head of the labour unions. They were overthrown in 1928, the year which marked Stalin's emergence as unquestioned leader of the Communist Party.

Things to Do

1. Read about Russia just before the revolution; make a detailed list of the major social problems.
2. Study the life of Lenin; do you think there could have been a Bolshevik revolution without him?
3. Read more about Stalin. What major changes did he introduce into Russian Communism?

Books to Read or Consult

J. Carmichael, *A Short History of the Russian Revolution,* London 1966.

A. Cash, *Great Neighbours USSR,* London 1965.

E. M. Halliday, *Russia in Revolution,* London 1967.

O. Hoetzsch, *The Evolution of Russia,* London 1966.

Europe Between the Wars

Introduction

The First World war left Europe exhausted but hopeful. Democracy seemed to have triumphed, as was shown by the creation of new states; the League of Nations was established and promised to provide an improved international order. Nevertheless, in spite of a general sense of optimism that a better world was about to be created, pessimism soon set in as post-war problems emerged.

Financial Problems

At the end of the war the most pressing task was to revive the European economy. Factories had to be rebuilt and turned to a peace economy, transport systems had to be restored, merchant fleets built up again, and millions of former soldiers given employment.

During and immediately after the war, Europe imported vast amounts of food and other products from abroad at a heavy price. In return, however, European states exported little and consequently were deeply in debt, especially to the U.S.A. American financiers were alarmed at the extent of Europe's debts, and in 1920 the U.S.A. stopped loans. This put pressure on European currencies, many of which declined. Worst hit was the German mark, which in 1923 collapsed; even simple items in shops were costing millions of marks, of so little value was the currency.

The German mark became almost valueless in 1923—simple items in shops cost millions of marks.

In the 1930s it was very difficult even for skilled men to get work. Unemployed workers from Jarrow marched the 270 miles to London to protest to the government.

Like the German children in this picture, children all over Europe went hungry.

Economic Progress in the 1920s

The financial collapse that afflicted the mark also hit the currencies of Austria, Hungary and Poland. The League of Nations worked out plans to stabilise the Austrian and Hungarian currencies, while by 1926 Germany, France and Belgium had restored theirs. This steadying of the financial position led to a strengthening of the European economy.

American loans were revived and industrial output rose, until by 1929 it was about 10% ahead of pre-war production. In 1927 the League of Nations organised a world economic conference to discuss economic problems. The main conclusion reached was that tariff barriers should be reduced and world trade made as free as possible. Little progress was in fact made towards this end.

The 1929 Crash

This economic revival, which was shared by most of the world, was interrupted by the Wall Street Crash of October 1929. The U.S.A. enjoyed an economic boom in the mid-1920s, and on the Wall Street stock exchange in New York, financiers put vast amounts of money into industrial company shares. The boom, however, had gone too far, for in numerous cases production was outstripping demand. In 1929 many American manufacturers therefore reduced production and cut back on employment. Financiers panicked and everybody tried to sell shares at once, the result being a financial crash. Production fell even more, unemployment rose rapidly, and the U.S.A. entered a deep economic depression.

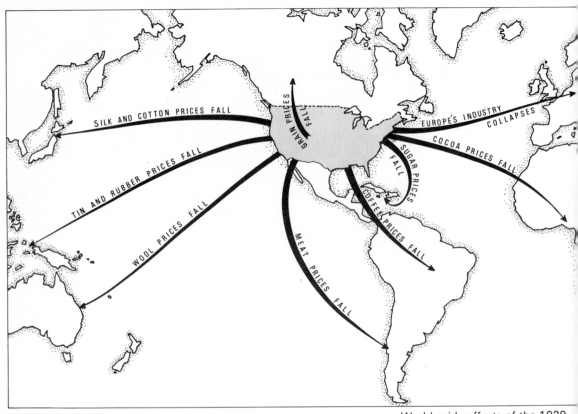

World-wide effects of the 1929 crash.

The crash had a serious effect on the European economy, which was dependent on that of America. American loans dried up again and Europe was dragged into the worst economic crisis in modern history. It affected agriculture as well as industry, it involved every class in society (not just the workers who traditionally bore the brunt of economic depression) and indeed it spread throughout the world. Between 1929 and 1932 industrial production fell by 47% in the U.S.A. and in Germany, by 30% to 40% in Poland, Czechoslovakia, Italy and Belgium, and by 25% in Britain and Holland. By 1932 unemployment had reached 13,700,000 in the U.S.A., 5,600,000 in Germany, and 2,800,000 in Britain.

During 1933 the worst of the crisis passed as financiers began to reinvest, governments put money into circulation by financing state building schemes, and production gradually picked up again. Historians disagree over which measures in particular lifted the world from the great depression; each country worked out its own salvation, but there is a strong body of opinion which argues that the depression would have passed automatically without any special measures by governments.

Mary Pickford, film star.

In 1896 Guglielmo Marconi applied for the world's first radio patent in London. He is seen here with his apparatus for 'telegraphy without wires'.

Rudolph Valentino, film star.

The Europe of the Masses

After the First World war the life of the European masses began to change out of all recognition. Education spread, standards of health improved and life expectancy lengthened. Also new and cheap entertainments developed that were aimed specifically at the masses rather than at the wealthy. Cinemas and professional sports such as soccer were typical of this trend. The heroes of the lower classes were often film stars like Rudolph Valentino, the heart-throb of millions of women all over the world. Comedians such as Charlie Chaplin, Buster Keaton and Laurel and Hardy were almost as real to the masses as their next door neighbours. The cinema became more attractive still

A scene from *The Gold Rush*, a film starring Charlie Chaplin.

when sound films were developed; the first successful sound film was *The Jazz Singer* (1927) starring Al Jolson. Experiments also went ahead with colour, and in 1928 Walt Disney brought out his first 'Mickey Mouse' film in colour.

Many other leisure activities spread, but tended to be the pastimes of the lower middle classes rather than the working classes. Mass-produced motor cars became available; gramophones could be bought; more and more programmes were broadcast on the radio. People had more to do than ever before and enjoyed much fuller lives. The annual holiday became popular and the working classes as well as the middle classes flocked to seaside resorts such as Blackpool, Brighton, Southend and Scarborough. These were all signs of the rise of the European masses and indicated that in future many of the activities once restricted to the rich were opening up to the man in the street.

Another important social change was the emancipation of women, which took place in many parts of the western world.

Emmeline Pankhurst (1858–1928). Leader of the British movement for female suffrage; in 1903 she founded the Women's Social and Political Union which agitated for votes for women; she spent several periods in prison, but called off the suffragette campaign when the First World war broke out; when partial female suffrage was granted in 1918 she joined the Conservative Party, and died just before full voting rights were granted in 1928.

Demonstrating suffragettes arrested in London, 1914.

A convoy of trucks, under military guard, leaves the London docks during the general strike.

Women increasingly were seeking release from slavery to the kitchen sink and from their status as second-class citizens. The movement took several forms, but laid special stress on the demand for the vote. In several western countries, women's organisations held protest meetings, marches and other demonstrations in support of votes for women. Their success is reflected in the fact that between 1915 and 1921 the vote was granted to women in Austria, Britain, Bulgaria, Czechoslovakia, Denmark, Germany, Holland, Luxembourg, Poland, Russia, and Sweden.

The Masses and 'Traditional' Europe

In spite of economic problems the condition of the masses was gradually improving. Nevertheless they still felt set apart from 'traditional' Europe. Industrial workers in particular saw themselves as an exploited group, and the general strike in Britain in 1926 showed that bitter class conflict was never far below the surface; this applied to most of Europe.

The urban masses especially rejected 'traditional' Europe. They saw traditional religion as the religion of the well-to-do. They considered higher education the preserve of the wealthy. They went to the cinema, not to the theatre. They listened to popular songs and jazz, not to opera and the classics, and they read the sensational press, not the serious newspapers.

Politically this rejection of traditional Europe was shown in the lack of support given by the masses to orthodox political parties, which were mainly middle class in character. The crises of the 1920s, and above all the great crash from 1929 to

At Kitty Hawk, in North Carolina, the Wright brothers achieved a flight of twelve seconds in their aeroplane the *Kitty Hawk*, 1903.

1932, demolished the wealth of many middle class people and alienated them too from existing political parties which had failed to solve the crises. When dictators stepped forward to fill the political void, they found that it was easy to acquire the support of the masses by subjecting them to propaganda and promises of a better world. The disillusioned middle classes also swallowed these promises and, with the masses, contributed to the rise of totalitarian regimes. One important exception to this was Britain, where a strong democratic Labour Party was formed that succeeded in winning the support of the urban masses, who thus continued to campaign for their objectives through the established political system.

Other Forces for Change

Communications were improving as the use of aircraft, radio, telephone and later television, was extended. The effect was to force societies closer together. Once whole nations, or groups within them, were isolated by distance, by language, by class, by religion, or by race. Improved communications meant that

Alcock and Brown with the aeroplane in which they were the first to cross the Atlantic in 1919.

One of the first Daimler motor cars, 1886.

Karl Benz driving his motor car of 1887. One of the gentlemen in the background holds a penny-farthing bicycle, the other has a more modern looking machine.

A London street scene in 1928.

189

The London telephone exchange in 1883.

people of all kinds were brought into closer contact. Europe therefore found many influences flooding in from outside, especially from the U.S.A.; in return the world was more susceptible than ever to influences from Europe.

Scientific change also contributed to the decline of traditional Europe. In the nineteenth century European intellectuals were full of self-assurance, but in the twentieth century became full of doubt, largely because of changes in scientific thought. At the turn of the century European science (and indeed science everywhere) was based on the methods and assumptions established by the Scientific Revolution of the sixteenth and seventeenth centuries. In the twentieth century, however, a new view of the universe emerged which made the traditional one inadequate. Two outstanding figures in this movement were Albert Einstein, who developed the theory of relativity, and Max Planck, who established the quantum theory. It became clear that the whole of the physical sciences needed to be rethought and that the foundations of much intellectual activity such as those of philosophy, mathematics and theology, were far from solid.

In the realm of psychology Sigmund Freud developed theories which stressed the role of unconscious forces, as well as those of the conscious mind, in human behaviour. He showed man to be a far more complex creature than was ever suspected.

Albert Einstein (1879–1955).

Sigmund Freud (1856–1939).

In these ways and in others, the intellectual life of Europe in the twentieth century was revolutionised. This was reflected in literature, music, painting, sculpture and architecture, all of which adopted new forms. By 1939 European civilisation in many respects seemed to have lost contact with that of earlier centuries.

Political Problems

Democracy soon showed that it lacked the ability both to win mass support and to stand up to the enormous economic and social problems that confronted Europe. Indeed, in political terms the period from 1919 to 1939 was dominated by the struggle between democracy and totalitarianism. On the whole totalitarianism had the better of the day. In 1923 Italy fell under the control of Fascists and in Spain a military dictatorship was set up. In 1924 Lenin died and, as was said earlier, Stalin seized power and turned himself into a dictator. In the 1930s this trend towards dictatorship continued and by 1939 Germany, Portugal, Poland, Hungary, Lithuania, Latvia, Estonia, Yugoslavia and Greece had fallen under dictatorial regimes of one kind or another.

The reasons why democracy generally failed are many and complex, but the major factors have already been discussed. The economic instability of the period weakened the middle classes who were the backbone of the democratic states; dictators exploited discontent by offering strong government and great national achievements; the traditional political parties had little attraction for the masses.

Fascism in Italy

The rise to power in Italy of the Fascists led by Benito Mussolini (1883–1945) is a good example of the failure of European democracy.

Mussolini and his supporters, 1922.

There was a great deal of bitterness in Italy at the peace terms of 1919. When Italy joined the war in 1915 she hoped to capture Fiume from the Austrians, establish control over Albania, and acquire some of Germany's colonies. Although at Versailles Italy did receive some territory, it was not in the areas that she wanted. Many Italians felt cheated and regarded the peace almost as a national humiliation.

Immediately after the war there were strikes and heavy unemployment. In the south the peasants began to seize land for their own use and threatened revolution. To these problems the moderate political parties dominating the parliament had no answer. In the cities of the north Communists organised demonstrations against the lack of effective government. It was out of this background of chaos that Fascism arose.

Benito Mussolini

In 1914 Mussolini had been an ardent socialist for many years and was editor of the socialist newspaper, *Avanti*. The Italian socialists wanted Italy to stay neutral during the First World war, but towards the end of 1914 Mussolini abandoned this stand, broke with the socialists and joined the army. He fought until 1917 when he was wounded.

Like many Italians, Mussolini felt that Italy had been betrayed by the Versailles settlement. He was also disgusted at the inability of the democratic government to cope with the Communist riots in Milan in 1919, and at its lack of solutions to the economic depression. Mussolini decided that the answer was to form action groups to combat the Communist menace. In March 1919 in Milan he formed the first Fascio di Combattimento (fighting group). He established similar groups elsewhere and the Fascists fought the May 1921 election and won thirty-five seats out of the available 520. The Fascists appealed to Italian nationalism and won much support from ex-soldiers and lower middle class people ruined by the depression. The basis of the Fascist movement was action, and they attacked and murdered Communist and trade union leaders, burnt and looted their offices and publishing centres.

The example of the Bolsheviks in Russia only a few years before showed Mussolini that amidst conditions of anarchy a determined group could seize power. He gathered his supporters from all over Italy and on 27 October 1922 began the March on Rome. Hundreds of thousands of Fascists descended on the capital; the government panicked and resigned; king Victor Emmanuel III tried to persuade Mussolini to head a coalition government, but Mussolini refused and on 30 October 1922 was made prime minister at the head of a Fascist

Benito Mussolini (1883–1945).

government. The ease with which he seized power can be compared with the success of the Bolsheviks. Both filled a political vacuum rather than overthrew an existing government, and both seized power amidst political, economic and social collapse.

Steps to Totalitarianism

Italy did not become a totalitarian state overnight. First a purge of anti-Fascist suspects took place, left-wingers of all kinds being the main target. In 1923 Mussolini altered the voting laws to guarantee Fascist success in the 1924 general election. When the election took place the Fascists, aided by a campaign of terror against their opponents, received 65% of the votes.

Now that he controlled parliament Mussolini dissolved suspect political groups, placed restrictions on the press, crushed local government bodies and replaced them by central government officials. Command of the army was transferred from the king to Mussolini, and anti-Fascists were expelled from schools and universities.

Now came the final steps. In December 1925 Mussolini was made Head of the State and could rule without the consent of parliament. Also, in 1926 the Grand Fascist Council was created to select candidates for parliament; only these candidates could stand. By mid-1926 all opposition to Mussolini had been crushed and Italy was firmly in his grip.

Adolf Hitler (1889–1945)

Germany in the early 1920s also faced profound social and economic problems, and an attempt to overthrow the government was made by Adolf Hitler. Hitler was an Austrian who regarded the Habsburgs as failures, for he believed that they had handed over the empire to the Slavs. He also blamed the decline of the empire on the Jews, whom he suspected of plotting to weaken the empire and exploit it for themselves. He developed a life-long hatred for them and later wreaked a terrible vengeance on the Jews. He admired Germany and when the First World war broke out joined her army, not that of Austria-Hungary.

After the war Hitler joined one of the many small political parties in Bavaria, the German Workers' Party. When he left the army in 1920 he devoted all his energies to its affairs.

Under Hitler the party, which took the title 'National Socialist Workers' Party' ('Nazi' for short), made rapid progress. He organised meetings, spoke against the Versailles settlement, and developed connections with leading Munich families whose support lent an air of respectability to the party. He also secured

Children march in Munich carrying
the Nazi *Swastika* flag, 1925.

the help of Ernst Röhm, an ex-professional soldier, who organised a private Nazi army, the S.A. (stormtroopers) and had valuable connections in the army and in the Bavarian government.

In 1923 Hitler believed that he could seize power, for conditions were ripe. The mark had collapsed, the French had invaded the Ruhr, there was a threat of a Communist revolution and the government was unpopular. On 8 November 1923 he announced his seizure of power. The army, however, would not support him, the Munich authorities denounced him and the government in Berlin sent the authorities a promise of help. The next day Hitler led a huge march of his followers, but troops and police fired on the procession and Hitler was arrested. He spent the winter in prison where he wrote *Mein Kampf* (*My Struggle*).

The Nazis, 1924–33

During the mid-1920s the fortunes of the Nazis declined, for the economic prosperity of the period meant that people lost interest in them. Although the Nazis fought in general elections they made little headway. Their proportion of the vote fell from 6.6% in May 1924 to 2.6% in May 1928. The factor that brought the Nazis new support was the economic crash of 1929-32.

Adolf Hitler meets president
Hindenburg.

The crash plunged Germany into chaos, and the government
had no successful measures to apply. Public outcry became
intense and two parties claimed to have solutions to the crisis.
One was the Communists, who in 1932 had 100 seats out of
607 in the Reichstag (parliament), and who preached the
establishment of a Communist state. The other was the Nazis,
who attacked the Communists, the government and, above all,
the Jews. The government was so weak that in July 1932 a
general election was called. The Nazis won 230 seats and
became the largest party in the Reichstag. Hitler was now
a strong possibility for chancellor. Several months of wrangling
followed, until president Hindenburg decided that the only
answer was to appoint Hitler, on the understanding that the

Nazis did not monopolise seats on the cabinet. Hitler was made chancellor on 30 January 1933.

The Establishment of Nazi Control

Hitler established his dictatorship much more quickly than had Mussolini in Italy. A general election was set for March 1933, and, like the Fascists, the Nazis prepared for it by terrorism and propaganda. One week before the election a fire burnt out the debating chamber of the Reichstag. The Nazis blamed this on the Communists and called on the country to unite against them. When the election results were announced, however, although the Nazis had 288 seats, the Communists were still the third largest party with 81 seats. The Nazis formed a coalition with the Nationalists (52 seats) and banned the Communist deputies. The Enabling Act was passed, suspending the constitution and placing dictatorial powers in Hitler's hands.

During the rest of the year he made himself supreme. He eliminated the other political parties, appointed Nazis to leading political positions all over the country, and signed a Concordat with the Roman Catholic Church. The climax came on 30 June 1934, the 'night of the long knives', when Hitler purged the Nazi party itself. All his possible rivals or critics, including Röhm, were murdered.

The Spanish Problem

Another good example of the failure of democracy is Spain. She was a country split by deep divisions. Regionalism was strong, and Catalonia in particular sought a certain amount of self-rule. There were powerful social tensions. Town and country were divided; 'official' Spain (the monarchy, the army, the Catholic Church, and the landed aristocracy) was bitterly attacked by intellectuals who wanted to end Spanish cultural isolation and open Spain to influences from abroad; official Spain was also separated from the masses who regarded it as an instrument of oppression. There were economic problems too. Spanish industry and agriculture were old fashioned in their techniques and badly needed bringing up to date. Labour relations were filled with hatred, as industry lurched from one strike to another. In 1917 there was a general strike and for a time it looked as if Spain, like Russia, might overthrow the monarchy and all it represented. The army crushed the strike, however, and the monarchy survived.

As far as the masses were concerned, they took little part in the political life of the country. Most political parties were either middle class or aristocratic, and did not cater for the masses. The principal organisations expressing mass opinion were the trade unions, the two most important being the U.G.T. (the General Workers' Union) and the C.N.T. (the National Workers' Union). These two unions believed that the interests of the workers would never be served by accepting the existing political system, but by direct action through strikes and eventually revolution.

Spain attempted three political solutions to these problems. The first was that of constitutional government inherited from the nineteenth century, which lasted until 1923. It failed because there were too many political parties, governments were unstable (there were thirteen changes of government between 1917 and 1923), and the *Cortes* (the parliament) spent more time on party squabbles than on the country's problems. Spain fell into disorder. There were strikes, widespread violence and anarchy, and by 1923 she seemed to be falling apart. Constitutional government had failed.

In 1923 an army general, Primo de Rivera, overthrew the constitution with the king's consent, and established a military dictatorship. Many Spaniards regarded him as a saviour who could restore law and order. This he did, although he did not solve any of Spain's basic problems. He ran the country until the great economic crash of 1929–32. There was much opposition to his government during the economic crisis, and king Alfonso XIII dismissed him in 1930, hoping that discontent would thus die down. In fact Alfonso had removed the one man who could keep official Spain in existence. A general election was held in 1931 and it swept republicans into the Cortes. They announced the end of the monarchy, the declaration of the Republic, and the establishment of democratic government. In this way the monarchy came to an end, and so did the second attempt to find a system of government to suit Spain. The third attempt now began.

The Republic, 1931–6

From the start the Republic faced powerful opposition from the landed aristocracy, the great industrialists, the army (although some generals were willing to give the Republic a chance) and the Catholic Church. Anarchy was also widespread and needed to be stamped out.

In spite of these difficulties, the new government made encouraging progress. It announced plans for agrarian reform whereby private estates were to be taken over and handed to the peasants. Concessions to regionalism were given, especially by the Statute of Catalonia (1932) which recognised the Catalan language and granted educational autonomy to the region.

The 1933 general election, however, provided a shock. Right-wing parties, who had acquired the support of the Catholic Church and had banded together to fight the election, won the majority of seats in the Cortes. Republicans throughout Spain feared that the new right-wing government would increase the power of the Catholic Church, clamp down on reform, and perhaps even restore a military dictatorship.

This last fear was strengthened by Hitler's triumph in Germany that year, for it encouraged right-wing extremists in Spain. Furthermore, two right-wing totalitarian movements, Falangism and the National Syndicalist Youth Movement, rapidly spread and advocated dictatorship in Spain. In 1934 the government signed a pact with Mussolini which was aimed at restoring the monarchy.

Left-wingers of all kinds decided that if democracy were to be saved in Spain then they must strike first before totalitarianism was imposed. In October 1934 a general strike was called and fighting broke out all over the country. Peace was restored by the army which dealt ruthlessly with left-wingers.

Elections were held again in 1936, and this time gave victory to left-wing parties which had united to fight the elections. Conservative groups, dismayed at their defeat and fearing new reforms, resorted to violence. Once more all over the country there was rioting and killing. The government had no idea how to restore order, for it did not trust the army to remain loyal.

This mistrust was well-founded, for a group of generals led by general Sanjurjo was plotting to overthrow the Republic and restore a military dictatorship. Their *coup* came in July 1936 when they attempted to seize Barcelona and Madrid. The attempt failed at first and the army faced stiff opposition. It carried on with its attempt to crush the Republic, and Spain fell into civil war.

The Civil War

The war lasted until 1939. The right-wing rebels, who called themselves 'Nationalists', were led by general Franco, but the Republicans found no strong leader and broke up into quarrelling factions. Franco had the army, the navy, a united command, he received military aid from Germany and Italy, and so inevitably defeated the Republicans. He set up a military dictatorship.

The failure of democracy in Spain can be seen in a somewhat different light from that in Italy and in Germany. Democracy had little chance in Spain since the masses kept out of political affairs. The country was almost bound to be ruled by either a right-wing or left-wing minority; indeed this is what the

Francisco Franco (1892–   ). He served in the Spanish army and was head of the military academy at Saragossa; at first he supported the republican government, but quarrelled with it and was sent as governor to the Canary Islands; when the civil war broke out he went to Morocco and led an army revolt there; in October 1936 he became leader of the revolutionaries, and took the title 'head of state'; although he supported Hitler's policies he refused to join in the Second World war; his relations with the democratic powers were cool until 1953 when he signed a pact with the U.S.A. whereby Spain joined the western defensive system, although she did not become a member of N.A.T.O.

civil war was about. The conditions in Spain were almost totally unfavourable to democratic government.

The League of Nations

The League came into being in 1920 and its headquarters were established at Geneva. It was an association of states co-operating towards certain ends. It had two main goals: international peace through collective security (by which was meant joint action to protect weak states against aggression), and international co-operation in social and economic matters.

Guernica painted in 1937 by the Spanish artist Pablo Picasso. Guernica was a Spanish town destroyed during the war. The artist uses this picture to express his horror at the suffering and death caused by war.

On extended loan to the Museum of Modern Art, New York, from the artist.

THIS
LEAGUE OF NATIONS
BRIDGE
WAS DESIGNED BY
THE PRESIDENT OF THE
U·S·A·

BELGIUM FRANCE ENGLAND ITALY

KEYSTONE
U$A

An English cartoon on the failure of the U.S.A. to join the League of Nations.

To assist it in these programmes the League set up a Permanent Court of International Justice to which legal disputes could be brought, and the International Labour Organisation whose purpose was to improve conditions of labour everywhere.

A blow was immediately struck at the League when the American Senate refused to consent to the peace treaties of 1919. Thus the U.S.A. did not join the League. It has already been said that Germany was not a member; neither was Russia. In this way the responsibility for collective security was left mainly to Britain and France.

The Manchurian Crisis

Britain and France were too weak to enforce collective security against a determined aggressor, as was seen in the Manchurian crisis. In 1931 Japan seized the whole of Manchuria, and China appealed to the League for help. The League set up a commission of investigation which condemned Japan, but said that a new regime should be set up in Manchuria under the League's protection. The commission's report was accepted by the League in 1933, whereupon Japan resigned and continued her campaigns in China. The League was totally ineffective and unable to assist the Chinese government.

The Ethiopian Crisis

Collective security had proved futile against Japan; it also failed against Italy, who in 1935 invaded Ethiopia. The League organised economic sanctions against Italy, but reduced their effect by leaving out several important items including oil. Ethiopia collapsed and could only be saved if the League intervened militarily. This it was not prepared to do. In 1937 it lifted its sanctions, but Italy nevertheless left the League.

200

A French soldier watches German workers loading a train in the Ruhr.

The League of Nations should not be seen as a complete failure, for some of its economic achievements, which have already been mentioned, were considerable. As an instrument for protecting the weak against the strong, however, it was inadequate.

International Problems

Gustav Stresemann.

Germany remained the greatest international problem in Europe, particularly with regard to the reparations that she had to pay. Germany protested that the figure of £6,650,000 was too much, but was forced to accept it. Because of the currency collapse of 1923 she failed to pay her reparations to France that year, and the French, aided by the Belgians, thus invaded the Ruhr, intending to hold it until the reparations were paid. Full of hatred for the French, the German population undertook a policy of passive resistance. The crisis was settled in 1924 when an international conference at Paris produced the Dawes Plan (named after the American banker Charles Dawes who directed the conference). Germany had to pay a reduced amount and a loan was organised to help her to meet her debts. The plan was accepted and the French evacuated the Ruhr.

During the next few years international relations improved. The German statesman Gustav Stresemann and the French statesman Aristide Briand developed a personal friendship and common views on the need to bring Germany back into international affairs and so end the German grievance that she was considered an outcast. Better Franco-German relations were established by the Locarno Pact of 1925, which recognised the frontiers of 1919, and in which French help was promised to Poland and Czechoslovakia in the event of a German attack. The pact also agreed to Germany's entry into the League of Nations. Because this treaty had been negotiated with Germany, it was hoped that German objections, that the Versailles settlement had been dictated, would now be dropped.

More encouraging developments came in 1926 when Germany duly joined the League of Nations, and again in 1928 when Germany was one of the sixty-five nations that signed the Kellogg Pact by which war was renounced as an instrument of policy. Finally in 1929 reparations were again reduced by an international commission which produced the Young Plan. This was the last year of improvement. In 1929 Stresemann, the outstanding German politician of the 1920s, died. Also the great depression began, which overthrew the democratic government in Germany and allowed Hitler to come to power.

Aristide Briand.

Hitler's Foreign Policy

Under Hitler, German foreign policy became aggressive once more. The principles behind his actions are still hotly debated by historians, some saying that he had a preconceived plan of expansion, others claiming that although bent on aggression, he had no specific plan.

Britain and France answered German aggression with 'appeasement'. Neville Chamberlain, the British prime minister, hoped that if Hitler's demands that German territorial losses of 1919 should be restored were appeased by giving in to them, then he would abandon aggression. This view had one great flaw; it assumed that Hitler wanted only to win back the lands lost in 1919. Events were to show that this was not the case; he was intent on conquering vast areas of Europe.

Diplomatic Manoeuvres, 1933–9

Almost from the moment that Hitler took power German relations with other European powers changed. In 1933 Germany withdrew from the League of Nations. The following year Hitler began a rearmament programme. In 1935 he denounced the military restrictions placed on Germany at Versailles.

The extent of Hitler's aggression depended largely on the reaction of Britain and France, the principal defenders of the peace of Versailles. There were signs that these two powers were trying to form an anti-German front. In 1935 they signed an agreement with Italy to contain Germany, and again in that year France signed a pact of mutual assistance with the U.S.S.R.

Mussolini and Hitler.

Adolf Hitler in 1939.

in case either were attacked by Germany. This progress, however, was set back by two events. In October 1935 Italy invaded Ethiopia and her relations with France and Britain became strained. Also in 1935 the British government, without consulting the French, who became angered, agreed to the extension of the German war fleet. Britain and France thus showed that they could not act together effectively against Germany. The lesson was not lost on Hitler.

In 1936 he challenged France by putting troops into the demilitarised zone of the Rhine. The French government did nothing. This convinced Hitler that France dare not stand up to German aggression. Later in 1936 negotiations took place between Germany and Italy as a result of which Mussolini announced the 'Rome-Berlin Axis' signifying the closeness of German and Italian policies. The Axis became an alliance in 1939.

Germany and Italy grew closer still over the Spanish civil war. Hitler and Mussolini supported the Nationalists led by Franco and gave them military help. In contrast to this firm German and Italian policy, Britain and France adopted one of non-intervention. The inactivity of the two democratic powers served as another demonstration to Hitler that in international affairs they were of little account.

German Expansionism, 1938–9

By the end of 1937 German rearmament was well advanced, although not complete, and Hitler was ready to achieve some of his goals. His first step came in 1938 and concerned Austria, which he wanted to unite to Germany. A Nazi party had grown up in Austria, and with Hitler's support its leader, Seyss-Inquart, overthrew the Austrian chancellor and in March 1938 called German troops into Austria. Unification (*Anschluss*) with Germany was proposed to the nation, which under great pressure voted in favour. The *Anschluss* in a sense achieved what some Austrian-Germans late in the nineteenth century had desired, namely a greater Germany including themselves. Hitler, an Austrian, was fulfilling that dream. There were protests from the democratic powers, but Hitler ignored them.

Hitler now turned to Czechoslovakia. Three million Germans lived there in an area known as the Sudetenland. Their political voice was the Sudeten German party, which demanded self-government from the Czechs. In Germany the press took up their cause, claiming that they were being persecuted. France was allied to Czechoslovakia, and announced that if Germany intervened she would fight. The French position was badly weakened, however, when the British government announced

The British prime minister, Neville Chamberlain, holds up the Munich agreement and declares 'It is peace for our time', believing that war with Germany had been avoided.

that France could not rely on its support. A great deal of diplomatic activity took place, as a result of which France surrendered her position, and together with Britain informed the Czech government that it would have to give in to German separatism. In September 1938 a conference took place at Munich where the Sudetenland was transferred to Germany; the rest of Czechoslovakia's frontiers were guaranteed. The Munich conference proved yet again that in central Europe France and Britain were incapable of stopping German expansion.

Hitler was not yet finished with Czecho-Slovakia (as it became at the Munich conference). He encouraged tensions between the Czechs and the Slovaks, and when a Slovak demand for independence was put, announced that the Czecho-Slovakia established at Munich no longer existed. German forces occupied Prague on 13 March 1939 and the country was annexed. This outraged France and Britain. Chamberlain was especially incensed. So far he had given in to Hitler's plans because he saw some justification in them. The seizure of Czecho-Slovakia, however, had no justification but was an act of open aggression. It is interesting to note that Hitler, in crushing the Czechs, was doing what he thought the Habsburgs should have done to all the Slavs.

The British government announced that if Hitler annexed any more territory Britain would fight. The basic problem nevertheless remained; how could Britain and France in western Europe stop Germany in central and eastern Europe? To this question there was only one answer; Britain and France must form a strong alliance with the U.S.S.R.; France's pact with her was not enough. Negotiations were therefore opened with the Russians, but Stalin had no intention of being dragged into an alliance simply for the benefit of Britain and France. The Russians also conducted secret talks with Germany, and in August 1939 signed a non-aggression pact with her. The world was astonished to see Communist Russia and Nazi Germany in agreement.

Britain and France thus were left to stop German expansion unaided. Hitler was now involved in discussions with Poland over Danzig. In 1919 Danzig had been made a free city under the League of Nations, although most of its population was German. Hitler reclaimed Danzig and wanted the Poles to agree to full communications between Danzig and the rest of Germany.

Hitler addressing supporters, 1 September 1939.

Poland turned down the demand, and was supported by Britain and France who guaranteed her security. Hitler discounted the guarantee and on 1 September 1939 Germany invaded Poland and annexed Danzig. This time Britain and France stood firm, and on 3 September declared war on Germany.

Things to Do
1. Find out more about developments in communications (e.g. railways, aeroplanes, the telephone, the radio) and say what you think the major social consequences were.
2. Imagine you are campaigning for votes for women; write a speech supporting a cause.
3. Read about Hitler and Mussolini and write a character study of each.
4. Study the attitude of the Irish government towards the League of Nations.

Books to Read or Consult
G. Cudderford, *Women and Society,* London 1967.
H. G. Gelber, *The Coming of the Second World War,* London 1967 (Warne's Modern History Monographs).
W. A. Lewis, *Economic Survey, 1919-39,* London 1966.
A. J. P. Taylor, *English History, 1914-45,* London 1965.
E. Wiskemann, *Europe of the Dictators, 1919-45,* London 1967.

Molotov, watched by Ribbentrop (Germany) and Stalin (Russia) signs the non-aggression pact for Russia.

The Second World War and the Cold War

The War: Phase 1, 1939—40

Although Britain and France declared war on Germany in order to defend Poland, there was nothing they could do to save her. Within one month Poland was in German hands. The Russians had won certain zones of influence in Poland in their pact with Germany in 1939, and moved west to occupy them. Through the winter of 1939 to 1940 the Germans and Russians continued their expansion. The U.S.S.R. attacked Finland and Germany occupied Denmark and Norway.

So far no fighting had taken place in the west, and although Britain sent an army to France, all was quiet and people talked of a 'phoney war'. They were rudely awakened in May 1940 when the Germans invaded Belgium and France. Unlike 1914 there was no mistake. Belgium collapsed and the Germans headed for the coast at Dunkirk to cut off the retreating British. From Britain hundreds of ships and boats, large and small, crossed the Channel and rescued the British army stranded on the beaches of Dunkirk. The army lost all its equipment, but over 300,000 British and French troops were saved.

Long lines of British troops wait to be taken off the beaches at Dunkirk, 1940.

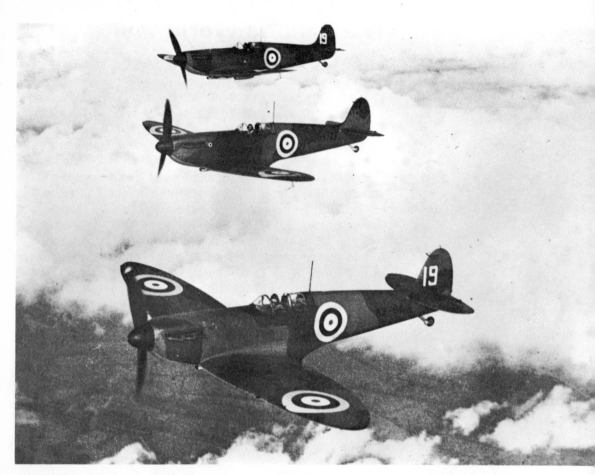

British *Spitfire* fighter planes in the battle of Britain.

Meanwhile the Germans were continuing their invasion of France, whose government was in a state of confusion. Britain and France had agreed that neither would sign an armistice with Germany without the other. Paul Reynaud, leader of the French government, wanted to abide by the agreement, take the government to north Africa and continue the war from there. There was strong opposition to him, however, led by marshal Pétain, who wanted to sign an armistice with Germany, establish a strong government, and restore what he called the 'moral order' of France. On 16 June 1940 Reynaud resigned and Pétain took over. On 22 June an armistice was signed. Many Frenchmen refused to recognise it and went abroad to continue the fight. One of these was Charles de Gaulle, who was supported by Britain.

Apart from the neutral states of Sweden, Switzerland, Spain and Ireland, Britain was the only country still unoccupied by

Suspension of fighting

omb damage in Coventry 1940.

Charles André Joseph Marie de Gaulle (1890–1970). He followed a military career, and in 1940 went to London and founded the Free French movement; in 1943 he moved his headquarters to Algiers where he established a provisional French government; after France was liberated, this government ruled until the Fourth Republic was set up in 1946; he had little to do with politics until 1958 when France was in turmoil over the Algerian question; he returned as leader of the country and set up the Fifth Republic with himself as president; he remained in power until 1969.

Germany in western Europe. Germany became even stronger when in September 1940 Hitler signed an alliance with Italy and Japan. Now that France had fallen an invasion of Britain seemed inevitable. Britain now had a new prime minister, Winston Churchill (1874–1965), who warned the country to be ready to face an invasion. In August the German air force (the *Luftwaffe*) began to bomb Britain and concentrated on airfields on the south coast. The battle of Britain had begun. Day after day masses of German bombers crossed the Channel and were met by British fighter planes, Hurricanes and Spitfires, which took a heavy toll of the enemy. The Germans failed to win command of the air over the Channel which they needed if Britain were to be invaded. Hitler then made a mistake. On 7 September he switched the bomber attacks from the airfields to London. A blitz followed, doing a great deal of damage to London, but it did mean that the airfields were left alone. Hitler's

Another view of the destruction of large areas in Coventry by German bombers.

German troops.

one chance of gaining control of the air had been to damage the airfields so badly that aircraft could not take off. The Royal Air Force won the battle of Britain and forced Hitler to abandon the idea of an invasion.

The War: Phase 2, 1941

During the winter of 1940–1 Hitler had to decide on his next step. He could, of course, still attempt an invasion of Britain, but the benefits of victory were outweighed by the immense effort involved. What is more, if he were tied down in a British campaign he would be dangerously weak in eastern Europe. Hitler regarded his pact with the U.S.S.R. as nothing more than a means of keeping the Russians at bay for a time. He was convinced that if Germany were to dominate Europe then Russia too must be defeated, for he knew that Communist Russia would not tolerate Nazi control of Europe.

Hitler therefore planned the invasion of Russia (the 'Barbarossa' campaign) which he intended to begin on 1 May 1941. In fact the invasion did not take place until 22 June. The reason for the delay was that Hitler had to help Mussolini, who had declared war on Greece but was being beaten. German troops conquered Greece on behalf of Italy, and also seized Yugoslavia for refusing to join the Axis. Now the whole of Europe was in

Winston Leonard Spencer Churchill (1874–1965). After a career in the army he became an M.P. in 1900; during the First World war and the 1920s he held several posts in the British government, but was out of office in the 1930s; in 1940 he became prime minister and proved to be the greatest leader in the Second World war; he lost the general election of 1945 but was prime minister again from 1951–5; he advocated strong ties between democratic states and hoped to see a United States of Europe formed.

210

The bombing of Pearl Harbour,
December 1941.

Hitler's hands. If he could defeat Russia and put her vast resources at Germany's disposal, then Germany, aided by Japan
in the Far East, could dominate the world.

Japan

Japan still hoped to create an empire as in the 1890s. Conditions during the 1930s seemed ripe. China was torn by civil
war, the U.S.A. had serious internal economic and social
problems, as did the European states who were in no position
to interfere in the Far East. Thus it seemed to Japan that it would
be easy to create an empire.

So it was. In 1931 Japan invaded Manchuria, and during the
next few years continued to extend her control over China,
against whom she launched a full scale war in 1937. The
Japanese government also considered attacking Russia, but
decided instead to concentrate on south-east Asia; in April 1941
Japan therefore signed a non-aggression pact with the U.S.S.R.

Just as Germany knew that she could not dominate Europe
without either coming to terms with, or defeating Russia, so
Japan knew that she could not create an empire in the Far East
without dealing with the U.S.A. By now the U.S.A. had strong

German gunners at Stalingrad.

economic ties with the Far East, and in 1932 had soundly
denounced the Japanese invasion of Manchuria. The U.S.A.
was firmly committed to preventing the Far East from falling
into the hands of Japan. General Tojo, leader of the Japanese
government, argued that since a clash with the U.S.A. was
inevitable, then Japan must strike first and eliminate American
sea power in the Pacific. Once this was achieved Japan could
gain control of the whole of south-east Asia before the U.S.A.
could rebuild her fleet. After much wavering the government
agreed. On 7 December 1941 a Japanese air and sea attack was
made on the American fleet at Pearl Harbour in Hawaii. Over
half the fleet was destroyed. The next day Britain and the U.S.A.
declared war on Japan: on 11 December Hitler declared war
on the U.S.A. The Second World war was now being fought in
three main areas; Russia, the Pacific, and western Europe.

German troops in Russia, winter
1941–2.

American marines plant the U.S. flag on the island of Iwo Jima in the Pacific. The island was invaded by 60,000 marines and was captured in twenty-six days.

The War in Russia

At first the German invasion of Russia was successful, and the whole of western Russia fell to the Germans. They pushed on to Moscow and Leningrad, but were halted there. Winter set in and played havoc with their troops.

In 1942 Hitler launched a second Russian campaign, this time in the Ukraine. He aimed for the Caucasus and the oil wells of Baku. The Germans tried to cross the Volga at Stalingrad, but met intense Russian resistance. Once more winter was approaching and the campaign came to a stop. Hitler refused the advice of his generals to withdraw the army before it was destroyed by the winter. This decision was disastrous. The Russians counter-attacked, and in January 1943 annihilated the German army at Stalingrad.

The Russians now began to win back lost territory. Moscow and Leningrad were retaken, the Ukraine was reconquered in 1943, while in 1944 Finland, Rumania and Bulgaria were forced to sue for peace and Germany was invaded. In 1945 Hungary surrendered and Russian troops reached Berlin in April 1945.

The War in the Pacific

Japanese hopes that victory at Pearl Harbour would keep the U.S.A. out of the war for a long time proved mistaken. American industry showed an astonishing productive capacity. Aircraft carriers were built that took the American air force to the Pacific war zone, and general MacArthur devised rapid, hard attacks on different parts of Japanese-occupied Asia. The Japanese never knew where the next attack would come and thus had no adequate means of defence. One after another the territories captured by Japan were taken by the Americans.

The War in Western Europe

Britain and the U.S.A. were divided over the war in Europe. The Americans wanted an invasion of France, but Britain wanted first of all a number of campaigns to wear down the enemy.

German tanks and troops in north Africa.

She wanted to concentrate on the Mediterranean where the Italians were mainly fighting and where the Suez Canal was in danger. The Italians were militarily inferior to the Germans and there was a good chance of success against them.

At first the British view prevailed. In 1942 a campaign (operation 'Torch') was launched in north Africa, from where the Italians and Germans were expelled by May 1943. In July 1943 Italy was invaded; she surrendered in September.

Now the American plan was put into effect. A colossal invasion force was gathered in Britain under general Eisenhower, who on 6 June 1944 ('D' day) launched the invasion, which landed in Normandy. By November France and Belgium had been liberated. All over Nazi-dominated Europe resistance movements spread in which Communists played a large part, and seriously harassed the Germans. In Yugoslavia, where the head of the resistance was Josip Broz-Tito, secretary-general of the Communist party there, the movement was successful and the Communists took over the country.

The Meetings of the 'Big Three'

It was obvious that Germany could not hold out much longer. The leaders of the main allied powers, Roosevelt, Churchill and Stalin, met at Teheran (December 1943) and Yalta (February 1945) to discuss terms of peace. These talks showed them to be hostile to each other, with little chance of co-operating once the war was finished. The only agreements were that after the war a United Nations Organisation should be set up, and the U.S.S.R. promised to help the U.S.A. against Japan three months after the defeat of Germany. On the rest there was disagreement. Britain and the U.S.A. wanted post-war Europe to be ruled by democratic governments elected by the people; Russia intended imposing Communist regimes on the countries that she conquered. Another conference met at Potsdam in July 1945, which produced little more than a hardening of the

From left: Churchill, Roosevelt and Stalin at the Yalta conference in 1945.

hostility. It was most significant for the fact that the U.S.A. and Britain were represented by different leaders. Roosevelt had died on 12 April 1945 and was succeeded by Truman. In the British general election of 1945 the Conservatives led by Churchill were defeated, and Attlee, the Labour party leader, took over the government.

The End of the War in Europe

In 1945 the Russians were invading Germany from the east and the Anglo-American forces from the west. Germany was being subjected to devastating bombing, as much out of a spirit of revenge as for any military reasons; her armies were in total collapse. Hitler was a physical and mental wreck. News came that on 28 April Mussolini had been killed by the Italians. On 30 April Hitler and his new wife, Eva Braun, killed themselves. On 2 May Berlin surrendered to the Russians and on 7 May Germany surrendered unconditionally to the Anglo-American forces.

The End of the War in the Pacific

Although by mid-1945 the Americans had captured almost all the territory held by the Japanese, there was still the problem of Japan herself. An invasion of Japan would be a colossal task, and it was calculated that the casualties on each side could surpass one million.

President Truman decided not to invade but to use a new weapon that had been developed in the U.S.A., the atomic bomb.

216

The German city of Hamburg after an allied bombing raid

The 'bunker' or shelter where Hitler and his wife, Eva Braun, killed themselves.

217

Hiroshima after the atomic bomb attack on 6 August 1945.

On 6 August an atomic bomb was dropped on the Japanese city of Hiroshima, and on 9 August another was dropped on Nagasaki. The destruction wrought by these bombs was terrifying. The two cities were wiped out, their populations were destroyed, and it was also discovered that the bombs continued to kill people long after they were dropped, for radiation poison spread. Weapons of this nature could eliminate an entire nation. Japan surrendered on 14 August. The war was over.

Russia at the End of the War

The U.S.S.R. did most of the fighting against Germany in the war and she suffered the heaviest losses. About 20,000,000 Russians were killed, the country was devastated and the economic achievements of the 1930s were destroyed. The U.S.S.R. still had two great assets. She had the largest army in the world and had conquered eastern Europe. She was thus in a strong position to create a Communist Europe.

The U.S.A. at the End of the War

During the war the U.S.A. was the main source of supplies to the allies. She maintained Britain and Russia with food, clothing and weapons. Her ability to produce war goods on an unlimited scale was almost miraculous, and never before had any country shown such industrial might. Because of her geographical position she could not be attacked and her industry progressed unhindered. She also dominated the war in the Pacific and did most of the fighting against Japan. The U.S.A. emerged from the war as the wealthiest country in the world, and the greatest military power, with the largest and best navy, the finest army, the strongest air force and, above all, the atomic bomb.

An atomic bomb explosion.

Britain at the End of the War

Of the allies Britain was the greatest loser in the Second World war. She had been in the war longer than any country except Germany, she had been able to draw on the manpower of her empire, and she fought in every arena of the war. She was, however, economically ruined. Her overseas investments were much reduced and she had heavy debts to the U.S.A. Her trade had almost disappeared and it was doubtful whether she could rebuild it to pre-war levels. Her hold on the empire was slipping as demands for self-government and independence grew, especially in her Asian and African territories. Britain's power had been founded on her empire and her navy; the one was slipping from her grasp and the other no longer ruled the waves. After 1945 Britain's claims to be a great power grew weaker and weaker. Her economic revival failed to equal that of Russia, Japan, Germany and France, and although she lost her empire she did not compensate by taking part in the major European movements of the 1950s.

Germany at the End of the War

Germany's domination of Europe was ended and she was partitioned by Britain, France, the U.S.A. and the U.S.S.R., who occupied their respective areas. No peace was signed and no terms were presented to the Germans as in 1919. Hatred of Germany was already deep throughout Europe, and it was intensified when the full story of the conduct of the Nazis and

Russian and American soldiers meet in Germany, 1945.

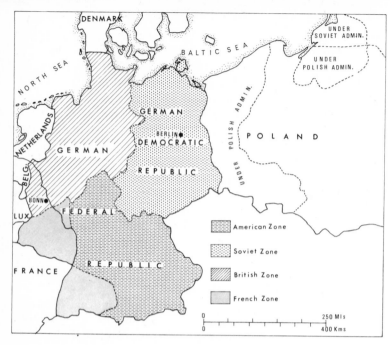

Germany after the Second World war.

their servants came to light. Concentration camps were relieved and evidence appeared of starvation, disease and torture. The Jews had been exterminated in gas chambers at Treblinka, Auschwitz, Dachau and Belsen, and it is thought that about 6,000,000 were executed. From 1945 to 1946 trials of twenty-two Nazi war criminals were held at Nuremberg by an international court; twelve were condemned to death, seven received prison sentences and three were released.

American president Truman (right) and Russian leader Stalin (left).

The 'Cold War'

Soon after 1945 a 'cold war' broke out between the U.S.S.R. and the western powers. One reason was that the death of Roosevelt and the appearance of Truman as president resulted in a change of American policy. Roosevelt had hoped that the U.S.A. and the U.S.S.R. could establish close relations and act together as international policemen to preserve world peace. Truman took a different view. He was anti-Communist and suspected the U.S.S.R. of being the centre of a world-wide movement to establish Communist regimes wherever possible. He set out to prevent this.

Stalin similarly thought that there was a capitalist plot to overthrow Communism. The U.S.S.R., so he thought, was in a dangerously weak position for the ravages of war had left her almost exhausted. Stalin feared that the western powers would be tempted to attack the U.S.S.R., and possibly use the atomic bomb, in an attempt to overthrow Communism there. The

Prisoners in the German concentration camp at Belsen.

U.S.S.R. thus imposed Communist governments in eastern Europe; in Bulgaria, Rumania, Albania and Poland from 1944–5, in Hungary in 1947, in Czechoslovakia in 1948 and in Russian-occupied Germany in 1949. The Americans saw this as proof of the existence of the Communist 'plot'. Certainly it agreed with Russia's desire for a Communist Europe, but it was just as much a programme of self-defence by the U.S.S.R.; she was trying to erect a line of pro-Russian states between herself and hostile western Europe.

The reaction of the west was one of fear, and in 1949 the North Atlantic Treaty Organisation was formed. Its members were Britain, France, Belgium, Holland, Italy, Portugal, Denmark, Iceland and Norway in Europe, and the U.S.A. and Canada outside Europe. It was later joined by Greece and Turkey in 1952, and by West Germany in 1955. The alliance put a belt of states across Europe as a barrier to the spread of Communism. Between this line and Communist Europe were the neutral states of Sweden, Finland, Switzerland, Austria and Yugoslavia. It was hoped that they would act as 'buffer' states to keep the N.A.T.O. countries and Communist Europe apart. The device worked, for there were no clashes except in the case of Germany, and especially Berlin.

The Berlin Crisis, 1948

Berlin, well inside the Russian zone of Germany, was shared by the U.S.A., the U.S.S.R., Britain and France. The U.S.S.R.

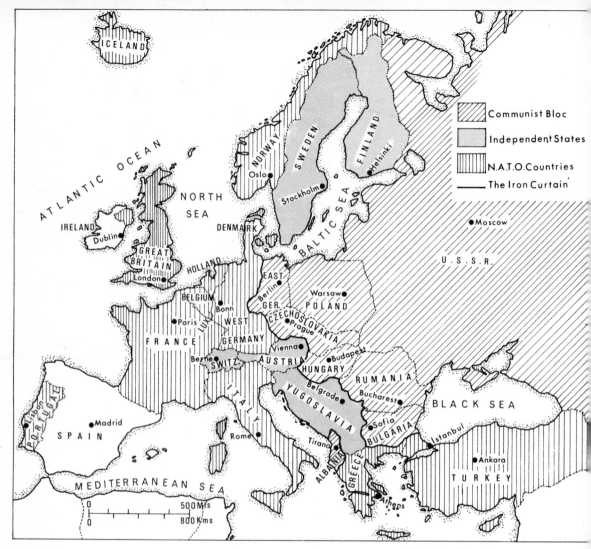

'Cold War' Europe.

saw it as a western outpost and in July 1948 cut off all land communications between Berlin and the west. International tension rose dramatically and even war seemed a possibility. An airlift of supplies into Berlin was organised, and day by day aircraft (one every five minutes) flew along a narrow route which the Russians recognised, and kept the French, British and American sectors of Berlin supplied. The airlift lasted until May 1949 when the U.S.S.R. backed down.

The results of the Berlin crisis were threefold. First, it showed that the powers wanted to keep the situation 'cold'. It could easily have led to war, but neither side wanted this. Indeed the Russians themselves helped to keep the crisis under control by joining the other powers in using their wireless stations to

The airlift of supplies into Berlin.

guide the western aircraft along the route into Berlin. The second effect was that the western powers organised their zones of Germany into a state, the Federal Republic of Germany (West Germany), in May 1949; the Russians replied by setting up the German Democratic Republic (East Germany) in October 1949. The third result was that the crisis encouraged the formation of N.A.T.O.

The Korean War

Another crisis that could have led to world war was the war in Korea from 1950 to 1953. By the end of 1948 Korea was divided between a Communist state in the north and an

American tank and troops in Korea.

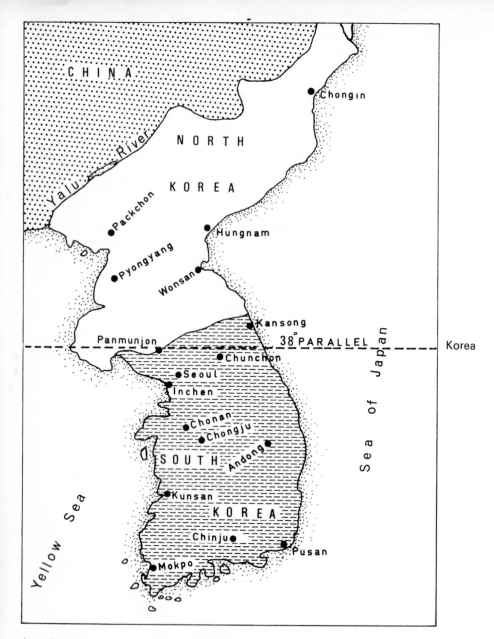

American-protected regime in the south. The border was the
38th parallel.

In June 1950 the Communists attacked the south, and the
United Nations condemned the invasion. The U.S.A. undertook
to restore the frontier on behalf of the United Nations, and
although she was assisted by other countries, she did most of
the fighting. American intervention turned the tide, and in
October 1950 the North Koreans were pushed back across the
38th parallel and their capital, Pyongyang, was captured.

224

At this point Communist China stepped in and sent hundreds of thousands of 'volunteers' to assist the North Koreans. The U.S.A. had to decide whether to limit the war to Korea or to carry it into China. General MacArthur, commander of the American troops, wanted to fight China; America's allies, especially Britain, urged Truman to keep the war limited. Truman decided on the latter course and the war remained a Korean war. This confirmed the pattern set during the Berlin problem whereby crises were kept under control so that the 'cold' war should not become 'hot'.

Things to Do

1. What major differences can you find between the conduct of war in the two World wars?
2. Compare the treatment of Germany in 1945 with that in 1919.
3. Read more about the 'cold' war in Europe; to what extent do you think the fears of both sides were justified?
4. Make a list of the countries in the major alliances, find their position on a map, and see where neutral countries lie in relation to them.

Books to Read or Consult

E. Luard, *The Cold War: a Reappraisal,* London 1964.
R. R. Sellman, *The Second World War,* London 1964.
A. Werth, *Russia at War, 1941-5,* London 1965.
C. Wilmot, *The Struggle for Europe,* London 1967.

Europe and the World, 1945–60

Truman and Marshall.

The Economic Reconstruction of Europe

The devastation left by the Second World war far surpassed that left by the First. The bitter economic experiences of Europe after the First World war had shown how necessary it was to restore a strong economy as soon as possible. Even more so than in 1919, Europe in 1945 was dependent on American help. It was provided on a lavish scale, for general Marshall, the American secretary of state, organised the European Recovery Programme (which was operated through the Organisation for European Economic Co-operation). This provided a generous supply of dollars and helped to organise co-operation in trade between the European states. It did not succeed, however, in the important task of achieving co-operation in production. Production still went ahead on a national basis and threatened to lead to the old problem of over-production in certain items. The Marshall Plan was also offered to the U.S.S.R. and to eastern Europe, but it was turned down.

The European Coal and Steel Community

The dangers involved in the failure to co-ordinate production were seen in 1950 when a recession set in throughout Europe, especially in the iron and steel industries. Jean Monnet, head of France's industrial modernisation schemes, proposed a European market without tariffs or trade barriers where national industries would thus have to be efficient if they were to compete in the international market. He wanted to apply this first to the basic industries of iron and coal. He was supported by Robert Schuman, the French foreign minister, who formulated a plan (named after him) for certain countries to supply coal and steel to each other on 'identical terms' (i.e. nobody was to receive special advantages). The E.C.S.C. was formed in 1952 and came into effect in 1953. Germany, France, Italy, Holland, Belgium and Luxembourg joined. The E.C.S.C. could regulate prices and production levels to fit the needs of the market. This plan was a first step towards co-operation in production as well as in trade.

Robert Schuman, French foreign minister.

The European Economic Community

By the mid-1950s the economies of most west European states were flourishing. The E.C.S.C. nations wished to extend their economic links and signed the treaty of Rome in 1957, which set up the European Economic Community (the Common Market). The E.E.C. was to remove all tariffs and other trade barriers between member states within fifteen years; it was also

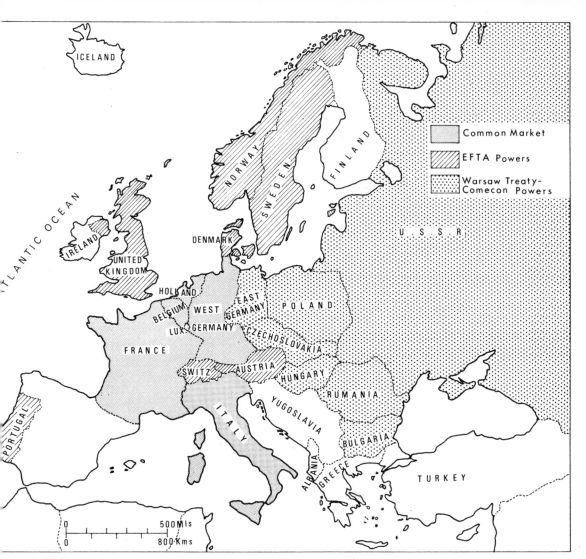

Europe in 1964.

to create standard tariffs between the E.E.C. and the rest of the world. The E.E.C. states were to have common policies on money, prices and wages. The treaty of Rome also stated that economic union was eventually to be followed by political federation.

Although the E.E.C. made considerable economic progress during the 1960s, in three of its main purposes it made little headway. It took no significant steps towards political federation and the nation states remained as powerful as ever. It failed to establish E.E.C. industrial concerns; industry remained organised primarily on a national basis. Finally, it did not manage to reduce the involvement of American finance in European business, and America's share of trade in the E.E.C. steadily increased.

The United Nations building in New York.

The European Free Trade Area

So far Britain had kept out of European movements and had concentrated more on her ties with the Commonwealth. Nevertheless she needed more trade with the wealthy Common Market. Britain therefore proposed a free trade agreement by which she and other European states would be linked to the Common Market. The plan came to nothing. In 1959, however, Britain established the European Free Trade Area with Norway, Sweden, Denmark, Portugal, Switzerland and Austria. The E.F.T.A. gradually abolished tariffs between its members, but made no plans for economic integration on the pattern of the Common Market. The E.F.T.A. failed to solve Britain's trade problems, however, and in 1961 she applied for admission to the Common Market. She was turned down because of French

United Nations emblem.

228

The General Assembly of the
U.N.O. in session.

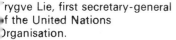

Trygve Lie, first secretary-general
of the United Nations
Organisation.

opposition. The French government felt that Britain was closely
linked to the U.S.A., and saw a threat of American influence
within the Common Market if Britain joined.

The Council of Europe

The E.E.C. was not the only attempt at the political integ-
ration of Europe. In 1948 a congress of movement towards
European political unity had met at the Hague, and in 1949 the
Council of Europe was formed. It included Britain, France,
Denmark, Belgium, Ireland, Italy, Luxemburg, Holland, Norway
and Sweden; it was later joined by Greece, Turkey and Iceland.
Although it set up a parliament at Strasbourg to discuss
European problems, it remained basically a debating chamber
without effective authority.

The United Nations Organisation

The chief experiment in international political organisation
was not on a European but on a world level. In 1945 representatives from fifty nations met in San Francisco to consider a replacement for the League of Nations. They founded the United
Nations Organisation, which was eventually established in
New York.

The U.N.O. had two main assemblies, the General Assembly
and the Security Council. The General Assembly was a debating
chamber where each member state had five representatives.
The Security Council, which was dominated by the U.S.A.,
the U.S.S.R., France, Britain and Nationalist China, dealt with
international political crises that arose. The Economic and
Social Council was also formed to promote international co-
operation and progress in education, economic affairs and the

preservation of human rights. The U.N.O. was served by a full-time secretariat headed by a secretary-general; he was elected by the General Assembly on the recommendation of the Security Council. He was responsible only to the U.N.O. and was not to seek or receive instructions from any single government. The U.N.O. also directed smaller organisations dealing with specific problems; these included such bodies as the World Health Organisation and the United Nations Educational, Scientific and Cultural Organisation.

The British Commonwealth

After the Second World war the old colonial empires broke up as their members won independence. This movement profoundly affected the largest empire of all, that of Britain.

Even in the nineteenth century Britain had known that eventually she would have to release her hold on the empire. Rather than see it simply disintegrate, however, she developed the concept of a Commonwealth within which nations formerly in the empire would form a free association of independent states with a special relationship. This idea proved popular in many parts of the empire.

Early steps were taken by granting 'dominion' status (i.e. self-government under the British crown) to the white-settled colonies of Canada, Australia, South Africa and New Zealand, all of which became dominions by 1914. Dominion status was also extended to the Irish Free State after the peace of 1921. This connection with Britain was never accepted with much enthusiasm by the Dublin government, which in 1949 broke away from the Commonwealth.

These developments were put into legal form by the Statute of Westminster, 1931. It announced that the dominions were fully independent, equal in the Commonwealth with Britain, and united by loyalty to the monarchy.

Until 1939 the dominions were those territories inhabited or dominated by European settlers. After 1945, however, Asian and African nations within the empire increasingly agitated for independence. It was inevitable that this would happen, and that the character of the Commonwealth would change as they reached dominion status and outnumbered the 'white' states. The leader in this development was India.

India

The British government maintained that the growth towards independence of the Asian and African parts of the Commonwealth must be gradual. Native civil servants must be trained and experience in government provided by handing over more

Jawaharlal Nehru (1899–1964). An Indian nationalist, educated in England, and leader of the Congress party for most of the period 1929–37; his opposition to the British caused him to spend several terms in gaol, but in 1947 he became prime minister of India; he introduced social and economic reforms, supported the Commonwealth, and kept India a neutral state; he failed to establish good relations with Pakistan.

and more responsibilities to the local populations. Each nation within the Commonwealth would eventually achieve independence, but it would be a long, drawn-out process, for in Britain's opinion some parts of the Commonwealth were more ready for independence than others. This policy was challenged by Indian nationalism, which wanted independence quickly, and not when the British government decided that India was ready.

Politically Indian nationalism was expressed in the powerful Congress party, in which Pandit Nehru, later premier of India, played an important role. Another leader of Indian nationalism was Mahatma Gandhi, who organised campaigns of passive resistance to the British from 1919 onwards.

The situation in India was complicated by bitter religious conflict. Most Indians were Hindu, but the country contained a large Muslim minority. In the 1920s, 1930s and 1940s there was much Hindu-Muslim fighting. Led by Mohammed Ali Jinnah, the Muslims formed the Muslim League, which insisted that whatever steps India took towards independence, adequate measures must be found to protect the Muslims.

A large measure of self-rule was granted to India by the Government of India Act, 1935. This provided for Indian government in eleven of the country's provinces; the central government was to be a federation of provinces and states and would be run by Indians, except for foreign and defence policies which remained in British hands. The Congress party attacked the act, and Nehru protested that it did not give enough political control to Indians. The Muslim League also rejected it on the grounds that it did not provide enough safeguards for the Muslims. The Muslim League now demanded an independent state, to be called Pakistan ('the land of the pure') where Muslims could live free from Hindu oppression.

Mohandas Karamchand Gandhi (1869–1948). Commonly known as Mahatma Gandhi, he was an Indian nationalist who, after a period abroad, returned to India in 1914 to work for the Congress party; he struggled for passive resistance to the British, reconciliation between Hindus and Muslims, and an end to the caste system; he was assassinated by a Hindu extremist on 30 January 1948.

231

A refugee family fleeing from Hindu-Muslim violence, 1947.

Ho Chi-Minh (1892–1969). A Vietnamese Communist who in 1941 became head of the Vietmin independence movement against France; in 1954 he became president of North Vietnam; he directed the Viet Cong forces against South Vietnam and the U.S.A. in the 1960s.

During the Second World war India fought alongside Britain. She gathered an army of 2,000,000 (the largest volunteer army in world history) whose troops were involved in every area of the war, but especially in Asia against Japan. More attempts were made, meanwhile, to solve the political crisis, but no answers were found. Britain continued to promise that full Indian independence was her goal, the Congress party still insisted that 'gradualism' was too slow a process, and Mohammed Ali Jinnah continued to press for an independent Pakistan.

In 1946 the British government sent a commission to India to prepare a new constitution in consultation with the Indians. The commission found so much confusion that it went ahead and produced its own plan. Terrible violence broke out again as Hindus and Muslims fought, and many thousands were killed on both sides. The 'gradualist' policy was obviously a failure; neither the Congress party nor the Muslim League accepted it, and instead of progressing peacefully towards independence, the country was falling further and further into anarchy. In 1947 the British government stepped in and partitioned India. The dominions of India and Pakistan were set up. Hindus fled from Pakistan to India, and Muslims from India to Pakistan. The refugees were attacked and slaughtered, and the death roll continued to mount. India and Pakistan thus won their independence amidst bloodshed and hatred of each other.

Sun Yat-sen (1866–1925).

Other Political Developments in Asia

The gaining of independence by India and Pakistan was only the first example of a general trend in Asia. The Indonesian Republic was set up in 1949, made up chiefly from Dutch possessions. In Vietnam Communists under Ho-Chi-Minh led the fight against French control. After a long, bitter war the French were defeated, and at an armistice signed in Geneva in 1954 the country was divided into two halves; a Communist regime was set up in the north, and an independent republic in the south. Malaya became independent in 1957, and was extended into the Malaysian Federation in 1963. Ceylon became independent in 1963.

China

China took part in the Asian movement towards independence, and emerged from the struggle with a Communist government, which launched her on a line of development different from that of India or Pakistan.

The failure of the Boxer rising proved that traditionalist China had no future. There was widespread opposition to the incompetent Manchu dynasty, and when the empress dowager and the emperor both died in 1908, to be succeeded by an infant, the monarchy was threatened with extinction.

There were many revolutionaries in China, but the most powerful was Sun Yat-sen, founder of the Nationalist party (the *Kuomintang*). When a revolt occurred in the army in 1911 and spread rapidly, Sun Yat-sen set up a provisional government. Many cities and provinces denounced the Manchus, who sent Yuan Shih-k'ai to negotiate with Sun Yat-sen. They agreed to set up a republic with Yuan as president. It was established in 1912; with surprising ease imperial rule was thus overthrown.

The Chinese Republic

From the outset the new republic failed to flourish. The government was weak, and Japan took advantage of its difficulties and seized the province of Shantung. In 1915 Japan put the Twenty-one Demands to China, which in effect would have turned China into a vassal state. On 9 May 1915 China accepted the demands with certain changes; since then the day has been observed in China as one of national humiliation. Yuan, the one man who might have held the republic together, died in 1916. China then broke up into a number of regions run by local warlords who fought each other. All over the country civil war broke out.

Sun Yat-sen, dismayed at the failure of the republican government to establish firm rule and resist Japanese aggression,

233

set up another provisional government in 1917. He appealed to the western democracies for help, but was turned down. He then appealed to the U.S.S.R., who sent advisers to organise and train the Nationalist army. Members of the Chinese Communist party (founded in 1921) also joined the Nationalists, who now challenged the weak republican government. Sun Yat-sen died in 1925, and was succeeded as leader of the Nationalists by Chiang Kai-shek.

A political cartoon showing the Japanese emperor, having made a meal of Manchuria, starting on north China for dessert.

The Nationalists

In 1926 the Nationalists went to war against the republican government and by 1928 controlled most of China; meanwhile, the Communists were expelled from the Nationalist Party in 1927.

The triumphant Nationalists introduced many reforms. They applied western ideas to government, financial and economic reforms were carried out, industry and communications were built up, measures were taken to promote public health services, and education was spread at every level.

In spite of such progress the authority of the Nationalists was menaced by many forces; there were two in particular. A serious external threat came from Japan, who in 1931 seized Manchuria. Japanese aggression continued throughout the 1930s and more and more of the country fell under their control. Another challenge came from the Communists, who concentrated on mobilising the peasants. By the early 1930s millions of people in rural areas had fallen under their sway. The Nationalist army attacked them and in 1935 seized the Communist 'capital' of Kiangsi. The Communist army escaped from Nationalists and fled to north-west China where it set up another 'government'.

In 1937 the Nationalists at last resisted Japan and war broke out. The Communists suspended their quarrel with the Nationalists and also fought the Japanese. Most of the coastline, which included 95% of China's industry, fell to the Japanese, but China nevertheless continued the war until the U.S.A. forced Japan to make peace in 1945. China emerged from the war economically ruined, fighting once more broke out between Nationalists and Communists, famine and disease spread, the U.S.S.R. marched into Manchuria and gave help to the Communists, and the country was again sunk in anarchy.

The failure of the Nationalists to restore law and order or to revive the economy pushed many people into the Communist camp. The Communists, who now held up the Nationalists as the oppressors of the people, launched an invasion southwards in 1948 and by the end of 1949 controlled the whole of mainland

Chiang Kai-shek (1887–   ). An ardent Chinese nationalist who supported Sun Yat-sen; he became leader of the Nationalists in 1925, tried to crush the Communists under Mao Tse-tung, but had to accept their support against Japan in 1937; after the defeat of Japan, civil war broke out again and Chiang Kai-shek was defeated in 1948; he retired to Taiwan (Formosa) where his government continued to claim authority over China.

Mao Tse-tung (1893—   ).
Son of a farmer he helped to form the Chinese Communist peasant movement in 1921; in 1931 he declared the first Chinese Soviet republic in Kiangsi; although pursued by the Nationalists, he agreed to allow the Communist army to help them against Japan; when the Second World war finished, fighting again broke out between Communists and Nationalists; Mao and his supporters declared the Chinese People's Republic in 1949 and he signed a pact with the U.S.S.R.; in 1959 he resigned as head of state but remained chairman of the Communist Party.

China. The Nationalists under Chiang Kai-shek retreated to the island of Taiwan (Formosa). The Communists divided up the country into six administrative regions and imposed strong government.

The question can be asked: 'why did Communism rather than nationalism succeed in China?' The reason was that the Chinese Nationalists ruled a country where the political system, the economy and social order all collapsed under the weight of war; amidst the chaos the Communists, who were well organised, thrived. India presents an interesting contrast, for there it was nationalism that prevailed. Although there was widespread Hindu-Muslim fighting, India was not faced with a foreign aggressor; the role of the British in India was quite different from that of the Japanese in China. Free from the wars that afflicted China, India did not face social, political and economic collapse, and the nationalists retained control of the country.

The Middle East

Once part of the Turkish empire, the Middle East was broken up in 1919 into a number of mandates; these were territories administered by a great power on behalf of the League of Nations. In this way Britain acquired control of Iraq, Transjordan and Palestine, while France received Syria and Lebanon. Another factor was that Britain, by the Balfour Declaration of 1917, supported Zionism, an international Jewish movement which aimed to create a Jewish national state in Palestine.

The reaction of the Arabs to these arrangements grew increasingly hostile. They saw the mandates simply as new forms of Anglo-French imperialism, and the spread of the Jews in Palestine as an attempt to take away land from Arabs. All over the Middle East disruption spread in the 1920s and 1930s as Arabs sought independence from Anglo-French influence and from the 'threat' of the Jews.

The Middle East after 1945

By the end of the Second World war the mandate territories had undergone change. Iraq had become independent in 1932, and Syria and Lebanon in 1941. Independence also was to come to Transjordan in 1946 and Israel in 1948; these two states had formed the original mandate of Palestine.

The greatest immediate problem after 1945 was that of Palestine, for full-scale warfare had broken out there between Arabs and Jews in 1937 and continued after the Second World war. There were some 600,000 Jews in Palestine striving for an independent state. The matter was debated by the United Nations, which in November 1947 voted to partition Palestine between Jews and Arabs. On 14 May 1948 the state of Israel proclaimed her independence.

Immediately she was attacked by Egypt, Syria, Transjordan (which changed its name to Jordan in 1949) and Lebanon. Israel successfully fought off the invaders, who signed an armistice with her in 1949. Neither side regarded the settlement as a peace; Israel wanted to extend her frontiers and the Arab states still wished to overcome Israel. This situation remained throughout the 1950s and 1960s.

Egypt

The most important Arab state in the Middle East was Egypt. In 1950 she had a population of almost 20 millions, whereas Israel had about 1 million, Syria about 4 millions, Jordan less than 500,000 and Lebanon just under 1 million. Egypt hoped to head the Arab nationalist movement, and perhaps even to create a united Arab state under Egyptian leadership.

Egypt had become independent in 1922, and allowed Britain to keep troops only in the Suez Canal Zone. The failure to defeat Israel in the war of 1948–9 roused the anger of Egyptian nationalists, especially in the army. Many army officers blamed the failure of the war on the corruption and inefficiency of the government. In 1952 a group of revolutionaries led by general Neguib seized control of the government, forced king Farouk to abdicate, and in 1953 declared a republic. The aims of the revolutionaries were to expel the British from the Canal Zone, and to release the Arabs from all forms of foreign domination.

Mohammed Ben Bella (1916–). An Algerian politician who fought for France during the Second World war; after the war he joined the rebellion against France, and was imprisoned from 1949–52 and from 1956–62; he was premier of Algeria from 1962–5 and president from 1963–5; he was overthrown in 1965 by Boumedienne.

David Ben Gurion (1886–). Born in Poland he settled in Palestine in 1906; he was a leading Zionist, and in 1935 became responsible for all Jewish affairs in Palestine; he was prime minister of Israel from 1948–53 and from 1955–63.

Gamal Abdel Nasser (1918–70). A professional soldier who fought against Israel in 1948; he joined in the overthrow of king Farouk in 1952, and was deputy prime minister of Egypt until 1954 when he became prime minister; he introduced many social, political and economic reforms into Egypt, strove to unite the Arab world, and became the hero of the Arabs through his handling of the Suez crisis in 1956.

It soon became clear that the real leader of the country was lieutenant-colonel Nasser, who in 1956 became president of Egypt. Under the Neguib-Nasser regime, economic and social reforms were introduced on a wide scale, and for the first time in centuries Egypt enjoyed honest government. The British were compelled to withdraw their remaining troops in 1954, British and French banks were nationalised, and in 1956 the Suez Canal Company was also nationalised.

This last action provoked an international crisis. Britain especially objected to her losses, and Israel took advantage of the crisis to invade Egypt. Israeli troops rapidly pushed towards the Suez Canal, and the British and French also landed troops in the Canal Zone; the British and French claimed that they wanted to keep the Israelis and Egyptians apart, but Nasser protested that they simply wished to restore their influence in Egypt. For a time it looked as if Egypt would collapse.

After five days of fighting a cease-fire was accepted as the United Nations strongly condemned the action of Israel, Britain and France. Under strong international pressure, including that of the U.S.A., they withdrew their forces. Although Egypt had been militarily humiliated, Nasser's prestige was

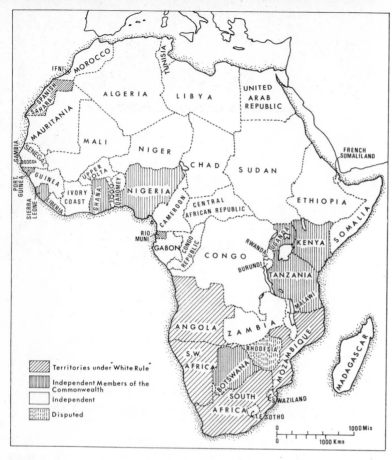

Africa in 1967.

higher than ever for under his leadership she had outwitted her aggressors.

The Suez crisis confirmed Nasser's power, ended the influence of Britain in Egypt, and left Israel still in a state of siege.

Conclusion

By 1960 the most dramatic events in the world were taking place outside of Europe. Nationalism and demands for independence, so powerful in Asia and in the Middle East, spread to Africa south of the Sahara. Ghana became independent in 1957, Nigeria in 1960, British Somaliland in 1960, Sierra Leone and Tanganyika in 1961, Zanzibar and Kenya in 1963. Still more African countries became independent as the 1960s progressed.

Again by 1960 the U.S.A. was playing a larger role than ever in international affairs. Her involvement in the Korean war foreshadowed an even deeper commitment to south-east Asia which eventually led her into the Vietnam war. When Fidel Castro seized power in Cuba in 1959, the U.S.A. was at first sympathetic to his government. As he increasingly adopted

Russian tanks suppressed the Hungarian revolution in 1956.

Communist policies, however, and opened his country to Russian influence, the U.S.A. broke with him and regarded Cuba as a dangerous Communist enclave which was too close for comfort.

Even the U.S.S.R. felt far from secure, for eastern Europe occasionally proved troublesome. Anti-Russian sentiment was so strong in Hungary that revolution broke out in 1956; it was immediately suppressed by the Russians. Her friendship with China declined, and in the 1960s Russia's suspicion of China became so intense that it forced her to seek better relations with the U.S.A.

Other changes were taking place too. The rise in the world's population assumed alarming proportions, and implied many political, economic and social difficulties for the future. Communications became more sophisticated than ever as television

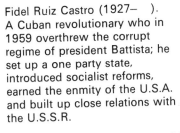

Fidel Ruiz Castro (1927–). A Cuban revolutionary who in 1959 overthrew the corrupt regime of president Battista; he set up a one party state, introduced socialist reforms, earned the enmity of the U.S.A. and built up close relations with the U.S.S.R.

239

President Kennedy of the U.S.A. shakes hands with the Russian prime minister Krushchev in Vienna 1961.

spread, space satellites were used, computers were put to work, air travel became common. The first steps in space travel were taken in the 1960s and by 1970 man had landed on the moon. In the rich countries standards of living rose to unprecedented heights, but in the poor countries poverty became more and more desperate.

Amidst all these developments Europe, especially western Europe, remained politically stable and enjoyed economic prosperity. No European state was a leading military power any more, Europe's empires had almost gone, yet Europeans were healthier, better fed, and wealthier than they had ever been. From this favourable position European states were faced with the responsibility of taking a prominent part in the attack on the world's economic and social problems.

Things to Do
1. Compare the UNO with the League of Nations; what were their chief similarities and differences?
2. Read E. M. Forster, *A passage to India* (Penguin paperback).

3. Read about Mao Tse-tung; compare him with Lenin as a leader of revolution.
4. Find out what main developments have taken place within the Common Market since 1960.

Books to Read or Consult
D. Bryan, *The Land and People of China,* London 1964.
C. P. Fitzgerald, *The Birth of Communist China,* London 1964.
G. E. Kirk, *A Short History of the Middle East,* London 1961.
K. Savage, *The Story of the United Nations,* London 1962.
T. Zinkin, *India,* London 1965.

Aer Lingus trans-Atlantic jet flight.

Glossary

administration: The governing authorities or the act of governing.

ancien régime: A phrase used to describe the privileged classes in Europe (but especially France) before the French Revolution; it includes the monarchy, the aristocracy and the upper clergy.

armistice: An agreement to cease fighting in a war.

bourgeoisie: The middle classes; the phrase covers everyone from small shop keepers to great capitalists (see below).

canton: The main administrative division of Switzerland; the cantons enjoy a large measure of self-government; there are 22 at present.

capitalist: Someone who owns capital (i.e. money, machinery, factories etc.).

centralisation: The placing of a large amount of authority with the central government, thus reducing the power of local authorities.

conservative: Politically this means a person who is opposed to extensive change in government or society.

Constitution: The basis of governing a country; it can be written down, as in the case of the American Constitution, or be based on tradition, as is the British Constitution.

Cortes: The Spanish parliament.

decentralisation: The opposite of centralisation (see above).

democracy: A form of government in which power is in the hands of the people.

dictator: A head of state who has absolute authority.

Diet: An assembly, usually in Germany, which had the right to discuss problems of local and national government; the members of the diets were usually aristocrats, upper clergy and representatives of towns.

Duma: The Russian parliament set up in 1906.

émigré: Somebody who leaves his country, often under pressure; in France it applies especially to those aristocrats who fled during the Revolution.

entente: A general agreement by two or more states over problems which previously divided them.

executive: That part of the government which carries out the laws passed by the legislature (see below); the head of the state is usually the chief executive officer.

federation: A union of states who remain independent over internal affairs, but combine for purposes common to them all.

guerrilla warfare: Attacks by small armed bands on regular troops.

indemnity: Compensation paid by one country to another, usually after a war, to meet the costs of damage caused.

judiciary: Judges, magistrates and law courts.

left-wing: A phrase usually applied to socialists of various types.

legation: Official residence of diplomats below ambassadorial level in foreign countries.

legislature: A body (often a parliament or some other representative assembly) which passes laws.

monopoly: Exclusive control.

nationalise: Establish state ownership.

pauper: A person (often a child) supported by charity.

proletariat: A Marxist term referring to the industrial working class.

radical: A person who wants widespread social and political change.

rationalist: A person who regards the use of reason as the way to solve any problem.

Reichstag: The German parliament set up in 1871.

right-wing: A phrase usually applied to conservatives of various types.

sanctions: In international affairs these are penalties applied by a group of states to another state to try and force it to abandon a certain course of action.

sovereignty: Supreme authority in a state, which can reside, for example, in the people or in a monarch.

Soviet: A council in Russia; the first soviets appeared in 1905, and again in 1917 when they consisted of workers, peasants and soldiers.

ultimatum: A final offer or demand.

universal suffrage: The right of everybody over a certain age to vote.

veto: The power to prevent a decision being taken or being put into effect.

Significant Dates

1763   Peace of Paris between Britain, France, Spain and Portugal.

1764   Hargreaves's spinning jenny.

1765   Stamp Act.

1766   Declaratory Act.

1770   Boston massacre.

1773   Boston Tea Party.

1774   First Continental Congress.

1775   Battles of Lexington and Concord; Second Continental Congress.

1776   American Declaration of Independence.

1779   Crompton's 'mule'.

1783   Peace of Versailles between Britain, France, Spain and the USA.

1784   Cartwright's power loom.

1787   American Constitution passed.
Assembly of Notables in France.

1789   French Estates General; National Assembly; Oath of the Tennis Court; Fall of the Bastille; revolution in the provinces; Declaration of the Rights of Man.

1790   Civil Constitution of the Clergy.

1791   Louis XVI captured at Varennes; French Constitution passed; Declaration of Pillnitz.

1792   France declares war on Austria; September massacres; French Republic proclaimed.

1793   Louis XVI executed; First Coalition formed against France; Terror begins.

1794   Robespierre executed; Jacobin clubs closed.

1795   Directory takes over in France.
Speenhamland Act in Britain.

1796   Napoleon leads Italian campaign.

1797   Peace of Campo Formio between France and Austria.
Robert Owen buys mill at New Lanark.

1798   Napoleon leads Egyptian expedition; French fleet destroyed by British at Aboukir Bay.

1799   Second Coalition against France; Directory overthrown; Napoleon becomes First Consul.

1801   Peace of Lunéville between France and Austria; Concordat between France and the papacy.

1802   Peace of Amiens between France and Britain; Napoleon becomes Consul for Life.

1804   Napoleon becomes emperor; 'Code Napoléon'.

1805   Third Coalition against France; battles of Trafalgar, Ulm and Austerlitz; peace of Pressburg between France and Austria.

1806   Battle of Jena; Berlin Decrees.

1807   Milan Decrees.
Treaty of Tilsit between France and Russia.

1812   French invasion of Russia.

1813   Battle of Leipzig.

1814   Allies enter Paris; Napoleon abdicates.
Congress of Vienna meets.

1815   Battle of Waterloo; Congress of Vienna completes its work; Holy Alliance formed.

1820   Protocol of Troppau.

1824	Trades Unions become legal in Britain.
1825	Stephenson's 'Rocket' runs between Stockton and Darlington.
1830	Revolution in France.
1831	Revolt of silk workers in Lyon.
1832	Parliamentary Reform Act in Britain.
	Mazzini founds 'Young Italy' movement.
1833	First state education grant in Britain.
1834	Robert Owen forms Grand National Consolidated Trades Union; Tolpuddle Martyrs.
1838	People's Charter issued by Chartists.
1839	Belgian independence finally established.
	Opium War begins.
1842	Peace of Nanking between Britain and China.
1844	Rochdale Pioneers found co-operative movement.
1848	Marx and Engels publish *The communist manifesto*; revolutions in Italy, France, Prussia and the Austrian empire.
	German National Assembly at Frankfurt.
1856	Peace of Paris ends Crimean War.
	Britain and France open war on China.
1858	Napoleon III and Cavour meet at Plombières.
1859	War between Piedmont-Sardinia (aided by France) and Austria; armistice of Villafranca.
1860	Tuscany, Parma and Modena join Piedmont-Sardinia; Garibaldi invades southern Italy.
	Britain and France capture Peking.
1861	Kingdom of Italy proclaimed.
1866	War between Prussia and Austria.
1867	The 'Ausgleich'.
1869	Suez Canal opened.
1870	Education Act in Britain.
	War between France and Prussia.
1871	German empire proclaimed; peace of Frankfurt between France and Germany.
1878	Treaty of San Stefano between Russia and Turkey; Congress of Berlin revises treaty of San Stefano.
1879	Alliance between Germany and Austria-Hungary.
1881	Convention of Pretoria.
1882	British occupy Egypt.
	Italy joins alliance between Germany and Austria-Hungary.
1884	Congress of Berlin meets to discuss Africa.
1885	The mahdi takes Khartoum.
1890	Bismarck dismissed.
1893	Alliance between France and Russia.
1895	Treaty of Shimonoseki between China and Japan.
	The Jameson raid.
1898	The Fashoda incident.
1899	The Boer war begins.
1901	Boxer Protocol.
1902	Alliance between Britain and Japan.
	Peace of Vereeniging between Britain and Boers.
1904	War begins between Russia and Japan.
	Anglo-French 'entente'.
1905	Peace of Portsmouth between Russia and Japan.
1906	Algeciras conference on Morocco.
1907	Anglo-Russian 'entente'.

1908	Austria-Hungary annexes Bosnia-Herzegovina.
1911	Agadir crisis.
1912	Balkan League declares war on Turkey.
	Chinese Republic established.
1913	Peace of London between Turkey and Balkan League; peace of Bucharest ends Second Balkan war.
1914	First World war begins.
1917	USA enters First World war.
	Russian revolution.
1919	Peace of Versailles between Allies and Germany.
	Peace of Saint-Germain between Allies and Austria.
1920	League of Nations comes into effect.
1921	Lenin's New Economic Policy.
1922	Mussolini becomes Italian premier.
1923	Hitler's 'putsch' in Munich fails.
	Primo de Rivera sets up dictatorship in Spain.
1928	Nationalists control China.
1929	Wall Street Crash.
1931	Spanish Republic declared.
	Manchurian crisis.
	Statute of Westminster on dominions.
1933	Hitler becomes German chancellor.
1935	Ethiopian crisis.
	Government of India Act.
1936	Spanish civil war begins.
1938	Austria declared part of Germany; Munich conference.
1939	Germany annexes Czechoslovakia.
	Non-aggression pact between Germany and the USSR; Germany invades Poland.
	Second World war begins.
1940	Fall of France; battle of Britain.
1941	Germany invades the USSR.
	Japanese attack Pearl Harbour.
	USA enters war.
1943	Italy surrenders.
1944	Invasion of Europe by the Allies.
1945	Deaths of Mussolini and Hitler.
	Germany surrenders.
	Atomic bombs dropped on Japan, who surrenders.
	United Nations Organisation formed.
1947	India and Pakistan become independent.
1948	Berlin crisis.
	State of Israel proclaimed.
1949	NATO formed.
	Council of Europe established.
	Communists control China.
1950	Korean war begins.
1953	Egyptian Republic declared.
1956	Suez crisis.
1957	Common Market set up.
1959	EFTA established.
	Castro seizes power in Cuba.

Acknowledgments

Grateful acknowledgment is made to the following for assistance in selection of illustrations and for permission to reproduce pictures in this book.

British Museum, London; National Portrait Gallery, London; Victoria and Albert Museum, London; Science Museum, London; Imperial War Museum, London; Wellington Museum, London; National Maritime Museum, Greenwich; Sir John Soane's Museum, London; National Film Archive, London; Wellcome Trust; Mary Evans Picture Library, London; Keystone Press Agency, London; Camera Press, London; Associated Press, London; the James Klugmann collection held at the Library of the Communist Party of Great Britain; City of Liverpool Museums; Bedfordshire County Council; Sheffield City Libraries; Halifax Museum; National Gallery of Scotland; Rijksmuseum, Amsterdam; Krupp, Essen; Historisches Museum, Frankfurt; Deutsches Museum, Munich; Markisches Museum, Berlin; Staatliche Museen, Berlin; Ullstein Bilderdienst, Berlin; Hohenzollern Museum, Vienna; Historischer Museums der Stadt Wien; Bulloz, Paris; Giraudon, Paris; Musée du Louvre, Paris; Musée Carnavalet, Paris; Bibliothèque Nationale, Paris; Archives Nationale, Paris; Musée Forbes, Paris; Collection Prince Murat; Collection Française, Paris; Musée des Arts Decoratifs, Bordeaux; Musée Gendé, Chantilly; Musée National du Château de Versailles; Musée de l'Armée, Paris; Musée Bonnat, Bayonne; Musée Jean Marmottan; Chartres; Museo del Prado, Madrid; United Nations Organisation; United States Information Service; Library of Congress, Washington; Yale University Art Gallery, New Haven; Frick Collection, New York; Metropolitan Museum of Art, New York; Missouri State Historical Society; and Culver Dublin.